HOW TO SWEET-TALK A

STRATEGIES AND STORIES
FROM A MASTER NEGOTIATOR

Gov. Bill Richardson

WITH KEVIN BLEYER

RODALE.

Rodale books may be purchased for business or promotional use or for special sales. For information, please write to:
Special Markets Department, Rodale Inc., 733 Third Avenue, New York, NY 10017.

Printed in the United States of America

Rodale Inc. makes every effort to use acid-free ♾, recycled paper ♻.

Book design by Kara Plikaitis

Library of Congress Cataloging-in-Publication Data is on file with the publisher.

ISBN-13: 978–1–62336–057–3 hardcover

ISBN-13: 978–1–62336–191–4 international paperback

Distributed to the trade by Macmillan

2   4   6   8   10   9   7   5   3   1 hardcover

2   4   6   8   10   9   7   5   3   1 paperback

We inspire and enable people to improve their lives and the world around them.
rodalebooks.com

To my wife, Barbara, who

for the past 41 years has stood by me

through thick and thin

CONTENTS

Bill Richardson,

UNDERSECRETARY FOR THUGS

I HAD BEEN SUMMONED TO the White House for one of the better reasons I could imagine: The leader of the free world was about to say a few nice words about me on television. What's more, he wanted me standing right next to him when he said them.

I was happy to comply.

As we settled into the packed White House Press Room, and as the assembled cameras powered up and focused in, the president took the podium: "All Americans have watched admiringly," he began, "as Bill Richardson"—*that's me!* I was slightly tempted to blurt out—"has undertaken the toughest and most delicate diplomatic efforts around the world, from North Korea to Iraq." Even though he spoke these words almost two decades ago, I still remember the pride I felt hearing them.

It was December 1996, and despite the date—Friday the

thirteenth—it was about to be my lucky day. Bill Clinton, my president and—at the time, at least—my friend, was about to announce to the entire White House press corps that I, the dark-skinned congressman with the surprisingly Anglo-sounding last name, was to be the newest member of his cabinet that "looks like America." Any patriot dreams of a day like this, let alone a *niño* from Mexico City who might never have even achieved American citizenship had his father not deemed it important to send his mother across the border to Pasadena for his birth.

My father wanted something for me he had long before achieved for himself. He wanted me to be an American, natural-born and proud.

Today's conservatives would call me an anchor baby, and they'd say it with derision—as if seeking American citizenship by any means, let alone the means offered unapologetically and indisputably by the Fourteenth Amendment to the Constitution of the United States itself, is something to be ashamed of. Fair enough—I was an anchor baby, but I was also a breathing example of the American dream. Because on that day in the White House, my lucky day, I was to become something more: an anchor in the administration of the president of the United States, at the request of the president himself.

Yet President Clinton used the occasion to do more than make the appointment. He also summed up the unique path my life had taken up to that point, as I'd bounced back and forth between high-stakes foreign rescue missions and devoted stateside service: "Just this week," he continued, with some amusement, "Congressman Richardson was huddled in a rebel chieftain's hut in Sudan, eating barbecued goat and negotiating the freedom of three hostages. Today, I am proud to nominate him to be our next ambassador to the United Nations."

President Clinton is not known as a man of few words. Yet it only took a few words for him to define me as a man of two worlds. *Negotiator. Public servant.*

Throw in *baseball fanatic* and *skeet shooter*, and you've pretty much got me measured. (You've also described my ideal weekend.)

The president was right. I am a contradiction. I allow that. I welcome it. I've often said that I live "between worlds." I'm of obvious Mexican heritage, but I enjoy the confusion my last name seems to prompt—the Anglo *Richardson*, a gift from my father, an American banker posted to Mexico City when he met my Mexican mother. My father set the stage for my embrace of both cultures, and both countries; while living in Mexico, he even paid both American and Mexican taxes, although he could have avoided the latter legally and easily. We lived in Coyoacán, not a fancy neighborhood, but my father made enough working for the bank that we had a chauffeur and a cook. I felt at ease with all my classmates, rich and poor, Mexican natives and American expats. Even as a young child, I spoke English fluently, but I dreamed in Spanish. My father was an aggressive personality, whereas my mother prefers a gentler touch. These days, I like to think I'm a happy medium between my father's occasional pugnacity and my mother's constant grace, but it may be more accurate to say I volley between the two as my mood suits. In a negotiation, contradictions can be useful: good cop and bad cop, rolled into one.

Todos en uno.

E pluribus unum.

So I took the president's words that day to heart. He was exactly right—I was as much in my element in the White House Press Room as I was in that chieftain's hut, between those worlds of serving the public and seeking compromise halfway around the world.

To be sure, a chieftain's hut in the heart of rural Sudan might be the last place any man expects to find himself, physically speaking. It is certainly the last place anyone would expect to *find himself,* metaphorically speaking. Yet, it is in those places where I have often felt most at home, where I have displayed my most unique, and perhaps most useful, talent: negotiation. As I often say, negotiation is about bridging the gaps between two different worlds. About reconciling contradictions. About finding common ground in even the most uncommon places. About striking a fair deal.

In fact, I am going to make you an offer.

Here it is: In the pages that follow, I am going to show you how I negotiate. I am going to teach you the lessons I have learned the hard way, in chieftains' huts and overseas embassies and foreign ministries and ambassadors' residences around the world. But put down that pen. There is no formal lesson plan here; that's not my style. Drop that yellow highlighter. There are no bullet points you'll be forced to memorize. Frankly, I haven't memorized them either.

This will, I assure you, be painless. I am going to teach you how to negotiate, and all you have to do is sit back and indulge me as I recount a few stories of my travels around the globe and my own negotiations with some of the world's most famous— and infamous—personalities. Hopefully our relationship from here on out will be what in executive boardrooms is called a *win-win:* You'll learn a few secrets of the art of getting what you want—usually from people who don't want to give it to you—and I'll feel the joy of recounting my more interesting, and occasionally absurd, high-stakes encounters with some of the most notorious and powerful leaders on the planet.

Not that I'm bragging. As you'll see, some of my stories are tales of success; others are of obvious failure. Regrettably, I've made my share of mistakes. The only reason I've hit a few home runs—and gotten a few people home—is because I've had plenty of at bats.

Nor, I must admit, were even my victories perfect. A perfect victory, or a perfect peace, is hard to come by. Sometimes the best you can hope for is an agreement of any kind—something that can establish a working relationship going forward—followed by an awkward handshake. (Come to think of it, a perfect victory is even rarer than a perfect handshake, which, as we all know, is next to impossible. I certainly can't claim one, and I hold a Guinness World Record for handshakes. But we'll get to that.)

Negotiation in any circumstance is subtle, complicated, and—despite that final imperfect handshake, that binding contract with a signature on a dotted line, or that flight back across the border—often without discrete markers of victory. So in the end, there are no hard-and-fast rules to live by. I don't pretend there are. If there were, negotiation would be easy. A computer could negotiate for us. There'd be an app for that.

When dealing with humans, with our human foibles, human self-interest, human egos, and human error, sometimes the only option is to throw out all the options and improvise. That's what makes negotiation so fascinating, and occasionally fun. As it is applied in real life, outside of the classroom, negotiation is about real-time compromise, about the art of the possible. It is not about finding absolute peace. (Perhaps that's why, though nominated for the Nobel Peace Prize five times, I've never won.)

Not all of my negotiations have made headlines, although some did—and not always the ones I might have wished. But I bring your attention to them here because each story has within it countless pivotal moments—teachable moments—about how humans behave in a negotiation, about what we demand of each other, and about what we're willing to give up to get what we want. The best I can offer you is a lesson by example. Or rather, by a dozen examples, each of which had countless moments when the negotiation could have failed or succeeded. Think of this as "how to negotiate in a million easy steps."

After the president spoke, I, too, took the podium in the White House Press Room that day in 1996. Naturally, I wanted to thank him for his kind words and lay out what I hoped to accomplish as the newest UN ambassador. But even I barely recall what I said at that particular moment, because just as I launched into my heartfelt speech, my friend Bill Daley—a fellow appointee, for secretary of commerce, who had also spent the last few minutes standing stiffly at the president's side—suddenly fainted and tumbled to the floor in front of the podium. C-SPAN has the tale of the tape; I had barely spoken three sentences before Bill's knees buckled and down he went, hitting the floor with an audible *thump*, moments after accepting his own appointment. To say the least, it was not his finest hour.

Nor, it must be said, was it mine. The tape tells my tale as well, and it wasn't pretty. Instead of leaping into action to save my friend from hitting the deck—I was, after all, the best hope for saving him, since I was closest—I stood slack-jawed, paralyzed at the podium, not quite sure what to do. C-SPAN caught Bill's embarrassing fall, but they didn't spare me either. As Bill tumbled down, their cameras lingered on me, frozen in place, as others jumped to Bill's rescue a tad too late.

Thump.

To this day, CNN's Wolf Blitzer, who was sitting in the front row, insists he actually caught Bill in time, averting a direct hit on the floor. That's not how I remember it—and Wolf, sorry to say, that's not how the cameras remember it either—although I cannot argue with another of Wolf's remembrances of the day: "Bill," he often reminds me still, "you didn't do a thing!"

That much is true.

What can I say? Although I like to think I have pretty good reflexes, first aid is not my specialty. Even on the baseball diamond back in high school, I excelled as a pitcher, not a catcher. Negotiation is my specialty, and at that moment there was no working out any agreement between Bill and gravity.

Whatever bargaining skills I have were developed often by accident and circumstance, in fits and starts, and frequently to my own surprise, but they've been finely honed by twenty years of high-stakes diplomacy in some of the farthest corners of the world. Over the decades, I've become something of a designated hitter whenever and wherever trouble strikes. I've talked down madmen in Africa. I've stared down despots in Eastern Europe. I've played hardball with fallen dictators, and softpedaled powerful hardliners. I've talked to terrorists. It's been said that I'm perhaps the only American whose regular commute is across the DMZ between North and South Korea. (In point of fact, one must fly over the Yalu River into Pyongyang through the Beijing airport, and only after visiting the embassy of the Democratic People's Republic of Korea back in China. But we'll get to that, too.)

To be sure, the bridges I've been asked to build have led to some uncharted places—Cuba, Sudan, Congo, Bangladesh, Burma.

My negotiation partners have often been just as inaccessible—Fidel. Saddam. Hugo. A Kim or two.

There was a time when, as a member of the House Committee on Intelligence during the Clinton administration, I had so many human-rights abusers on speed-dial that I was known as the Undersecretary for Thugs. I took it as a compliment. It evidenced my overriding operating theory—a theory you'll see repeated in this book—that we almost always benefit from talking, even to our enemies.

Whether I was acting as an official envoy of the government or as a simple private citizen on a humanitarian mission, I found a way to be useful in exactly that way—as someone who was willing to have a conversation with even the most controversial figures.

Often I was even more useful as a free agent, living between the worlds of the government and private humanitarian efforts. "Sometimes in diplomacy you need a fig leaf," as Richard Haass, then-president of the Brookings Institution, put it just prior to my appointment as UN ambassador. "The fact that he is not inside the administration but somehow connected to it"—between worlds, you might say—"is a big plus."

Negotiator. Public servant. Baseball fan. Skeet shooter. Fig leaf.

Guilty as charged.

Of course, none of this helped poor Bill Daley. Though I've since redeemed myself as a negotiator, the only "common ground" found that day was the ground found by his nose, in front of a packed room, live on television.

Bill got the last laugh. Later, when I jokingly accused him of stealing the spotlight during *my* moment, he insisted that he fainted because my acceptance speech was too boring. He's probably right.

So I grant you, I may not have been helpful to the newly appointed secretary of commerce on that day back in 1996, but I am fairly certain that I can be helpful to you today. In my negotiations around the world, I've gleaned some valuable lessons that can't be taught in textbooks, lessons about how people behave when the stakes are high, the degree of trust is low, and the ability to communicate is middling at best. Although not all of my negotiations have been matters of life and death, a few were—not exactly the usual curricula in Negotiation 101. I have lived a life where "getting to yes"—to borrow the title of the best-selling negotiation manual, written by two Harvard scholars, no less—might also include "getting to a shack in the Sudan" or "getting back to the airport before the rebel army shuts it down." I can assure you, that's a long way from the Harvard Club.

For their part, the books on negotiation that fill the business bestseller lists teach valuable lessons, but they are lessons that are useful primarily when the negotiators are balanced, coherent, and willing partners. Rational actors, negotiating with willing partners, hoping to strike a fair deal.

And while it's true that many of my negotiating partners in far-flung foreign lands were honest brokers who cared about the lives of their citizens, many others were narcissistic despots and power-hungry tyrants who cared more about their own skins than their own countries. (Actually, one of the first important steps in any negotiation is to determine which is which, and who is who.) The lessons I share have only one thing in common: They were learned the hard way. They were extracted, culled, and solidified while sitting across from some of the most unpredictable and irrational people on the planet.

But that's exactly why the lessons I reveal may be *more* applicable than the negotiation lessons you can learn from other books. Because let's be honest: Your life is full of unpredictable and irrational people. Your bosses, your spouse, your children, your neighbors—sure, they don't command armies or rule over countries, but they hold their own unique power over you, and have no scruples about trying to wield it at will.

Look around: You live and work with tyrants.

Schemers.

Narcissists.

So although most of my negotiating partners described in these pages may live far, far away, they may not be as foreign to you as it might seem. You may recognize their behaviors as those you contend with every day. Whether it be your husband, your wife, or your relentlessly opinionated teenage son or daughter, they mean no harm, and you love them, but you also know they don't work under any definition of rational behavior. There are no Robert's Rules of Order across the dining room table. And out in the world? At work? Buying a house? A car? A smart phone? Everything's a negotiation.

So that's my offer. Should you choose to accept it, read on. I believe you'll find these stories as entertaining as they are useful. And I hope you'll agree that the lessons they teach—while often gleaned from experiences halfway around the globe during my travels and travails throughout countries near and far—can be applied right where you live, to help you deal effectively with the scoundrels, ne'er-do-wells, thieves, thugs, dictators, and despots—and, yes, the loved ones—in your life.

The Clintons:

A CAUTIONARY TALE

I SEE YOU'VE ACCEPTED MY OFFER.

Rookie mistake.

The first offer is rarely the best offer—that's Negotiation 101. As my father told me a thousand times—in terms I, a baseball fanatic, could certainly understand—*never swing at the first pitch.* But you swung. That's okay.

After all, we all make mistakes. I've certainly made more than my share. It's a cliché that we often learn more from our failures than our successes, but it also happens to be true. Why? The sting of defeat hits us harder than the pleasure of victory. It's simply more powerful. *I'll never do that again,* we tell ourselves. *Just wait till my next at bat.*

Perhaps my biggest misstep, my most flagrant swing and miss—one that can be as instructive for you as it was for me—came in 2008, just as the race for the presidency that year was heating up. I tell myself I made this particular mistake, a rookie mistake by a veteran negotiator who should have known better—*me*—because in truth I wasn't the one doing the negotiating. Rather, I was *being* negotiated, by one of the best negotiators I've ever met: the same man who appointed me ambassador to the UN back in 1996. The same man who, famously, could negotiate everything, right down to what the definition of *is* is, and come out on the winning side of that linguistically mind-boggling argument.

So I tell myself I was outmatched by a master negotiator.

But the truth is, I bobbled an easy grounder.

In late January 2008, President Bill Clinton rang me with news: He wanted to see me again. Only this time, he didn't summon me to the White House as he had back in 1996—another fellow currently lived there—and his only shot to return was as the spouse of my competitor for the presidency. But so adamant was he that we should meet that he proposed—rather, he insisted—that he would fly to New Mexico so we could meet in person. He had a good enough excuse: He suggested we watch the Super Bowl together. On February 3, the New York Giants would take on the New England Patriots in Glendale, Arizona. It promised to be a good game. Although if Bill had his way—and on this day, he certainly planned to—the featured entertainment that afternoon was going to take place in Santa Fe. And it too would be televised. Yes, just like in 1996, he wanted to say a few words about me on television, with me standing by his side.

Then he wanted me to speak the few words he had scripted for me:

"I endorse Hillary Clinton for president."

It may have been Super Bowl Sunday, but it was also smack in the middle of the heated primary race, and any punter could tell what his visit was really about. I had dropped out of the race the previous month, and since then my arm had been sore from all the twisting it had received from all corners in asking for my endorsement. Hillary called. Barack called. Even Ted Kennedy rang me in support of Obama. But Bill came the most, finding a number of excuses to swing by New Mexico in the days after I had withdrawn. But this was his big pitch. We'd watch the Super Bowl, but the action would be in Santa Fe: Bill Clinton was making a house call, conveniently two days before the New Mexico caucus and Super Tuesday, to twist my arm harder than the rest and secure my endorsement for his wife for the presidency.

The only problem: I wasn't going to play ball.

I did try to manage expectations about Bill's visit—to anyone who might take an interest and to Bill himself. For starters, I instructed my spokesman, Pahl Shipley, to tell the Associated Press, "There's no message intended by this." This is just two old friends getting together to watch sports—as if that's something Bill and I had done a thousand times before. (For the record, we hadn't.)

Yet despite my apparent hesitation, or perhaps because of the poor job I had done of dissuading him, Bill still thought he would negotiate an endorsement out of me. He even told the local reporters there'd be a press conference, as he planned to get my endorsement by halftime.

I knew he wouldn't succeed.

Yet I still let him do it.

I still let him come.

Even when it got complicated, I still let him come.

Even when a strong snowstorm made it impossible for the

president's plane to land in Taos and we hastily made plans to relocate to the Governor's Mansion in Santa Fe—in other words, when I had a good excuse to cancel—I still let him come.

I still let a former president fly all the way to New Mexico, at great expense of his time, funds, and reputation—of blood and treasure, as they say in the war game—and I had not stepped in to stop it when it became obvious to the world what he was coming for.

Rookie mistake.

President Bill Clinton, who has at times been my friend and at others my foe, is a collection of superlatives.

Most everything complimentary said about the man is true. It's barely controversial to say he is perhaps the most natural politician of the modern era. To this day, he retains an unmatched ability to sweep through a room and charm each person he meets. When he finally departs, after tending carefully to each constituent—and we are all his constituents—for precisely the amount of time needed—no more, no less—to remind us, through a few perfectly chosen words and more perfectly chosen gestures, that life will be better after this meeting, he leaves behind the sense not only that someone important just stopped by, but also that something important just happened.

Even if it was just a handshake.

Yes, there's something about that handshake. He's got the best handshake in the biz. (And I should know. I have the Guinness World Record in most handshakes. But we'll get back to that.)

His speeches, even at their most winding and windy, render

even other speechifiers speechless. And on that measure he just gets better; his keynote at the 2012 Democratic National Convention, as loquacious as ever, had the rafters shaking.

Everyone—men and women—says that when they're one-on-one with him, they get lost in his gaze. They can't all be wrong.

Simply: He was born to do this politics thing, and he's better at it than anyone. He rarely fails to impress. Having lived much of my political life in the Clinton era, I've seen this firsthand. When I was being considered for secretary of the interior and he and I discussed the land-use issues I'd be expected to address during my tenure, his knowledge of the minutiae of Native American affairs was daunting, and came preloaded. I remember thinking, *Wait a minute here, I thought I was the New Mexican.* I consider myself a pretty avid baseball fan, but he once put me to shame when I introduced him to Carlos Slim and the two of them got into a deep conversation about the most arcane batting statistics. I couldn't keep up. Bill is probably the only person who read the entire North American Free Trade Agreement. He's certainly the only person who could cite it chapter and verse. From memory.

The man is a sponge.

He is also a man of his word, at least in professional settings. He keeps the political promises he's made, even when it's inconvenient. And on this front, he knows the value of the personal touch. After he chose not to nominate me for the job at Interior, he called me up.

"How you feeling?"

He already knew how I was feeling. "I gotta be honest, Bill. This one hurt."

He felt my pain, the way he can.

"I hear you. But stay patient. These things tend to come 'round again."

In my case, they came around twice. I did stay patient, and sure enough, three years later, President Clinton rescued me from a goatherd's hut in Sudan and appointed me United States ambassador to the United Nations. Then in 1998, he appointed me secretary of energy. He felt he owed me, and even years later—when others might have forgotten—he paid up in full.

So yes, Bill Clinton is the best natural-born politician around, and he is a man of many virtues. But flip that coin— perhaps the coin he'll be on someday—and most everything unsavory said about the man also has to be considered. It's clear Bill has been on the receiving end of a parade of accusations over a long life in public service.

Lewinsky. Whitewater. Worse.

Is all of it true? Again, that may depend on what your definition of *is* is.

To be sure, there is a megalomania common to all of us who run for president. It takes a big ego to assume that you should be the leader of the free world. And on this measure, Bill leads the league. He does presume that the world revolves around him— not least because, for a time, it *did*.

After the professional help he had given me over the years, it's no surprise that I got a reputation as being a strong Clinton defender, even when it came to his personal life. And he clearly appreciated the support. But even I was surprised by how effusive he'd be in his thanks to me. "I love you, Billy," he'd say on many of his late-night phone calls. "I love you, man."

Some years later, for reasons I can't quite decipher, as the Clinton administration was winding down, I began to get a sense that my relationship with Bill was souring. The count-less late-night phone calls talking about all manner of topics slowed to a trickle. (I realize how odd it may sound, but I missed hearing him tell me he loved me.) When I went to see him in the Oval Office to discuss my candidacy for DNC chair-man, he was brusque. "Terry's getting that," he said, speaking of his friend Terry McAuliffe. "I'm not telling you not to run, but if you do, we're going to have to crush you." When I tried to press my case, the president did the oddest thing: He stood up in the middle of my sentence, walked over to a bookshelf, pulled down a book, and starting flipping through it, his back to me.

I was getting the cold shoulder from the president in the West Wing. If the Oval Office had had an ejector seat, I'm pretty sure he would have launched me onto the South Lawn. After a few moments of awkward silence, I picked up my things and left.

There have been moments of reprieve. A couple years later, we met up in Acapulco. Hillary and Bill were vacationing there, and my wife, Barbara, and I joined them. The four of us had a nice lunch full of laughs and grand plans, like old times. I also brought the world's richest man and a dear friend from my childhood, Carlos Slim, to meet the president. They were like little kids trying to outdo each other at baseball trivia. Slim later contributed heavily to the Clinton Foundation. But even through all that, I knew by then not to rely on that feeling of bonhomie. Our relationship had been hot and cold—and get-ting colder generally—and I had grown used to that.

So in 2008, I can't say I was surprised when he reached out to me during his wife's tight battle with Senator Obama—a battle I had withdrawn from myself only a month prior—and insisted that we enjoy a nice snowy afternoon in Santa Fe watching the

Super Bowl with cold cuts, chips and salsa, and a dozen of our closest reporters. As halftime approached—and with it, the expected press conference—Bill still hadn't procured my endorsement. I leveled with him. "Bill, look. If *you* were running, I'd endorse you. But why should I endorse Hillary?" I had real reservations about the people she would bring in: the same old same old, as I saw it. It was clear he took my reluctance as a personal affront; to approve of Hillary is to approve of Bill. They come as a team. Still, I didn't find his counterarguments compelling. At halftime, instead of calling off the press conference, we invited in the photographers for thirty of the most awkward minutes of my life. When the assembled reporters asked us about what we were discussing, I let Bill do most of the talking—not my usual modus operandi. "The Giants have been great today," he said, ignoring the elephant in the room. "The defense has been unbelievable." When a reporter finally asked a direct question about the political race and Hillary's chances, all Bill could muster was "I hope she's going to win. . . . New Mexico has been very good to me. I love it here."

New Mexico may have been good to him, but I doubt he was loving New Mexico's governor at that moment. I was shocked that he didn't stand up, take a book off the shelf, and pretend to read. Heck, even I was wishing I had an ejector seat of my own. Not for him—for *me*. I wanted to be anywhere but there.

The game ended. The Giants won. The reporters left.

In the days that followed, Bill made other motions to pry an endorsement out of me. I learned later that he even asked Henry Cisneros, who had worked with Clinton as housing and urban development secretary, to intervene. "He thought I could deliver you," Henry told me.

"Why?"

"I guess he thought we spoke the same language."

"Politics?"

"Spanish."

Hey, I can't blame Bill. Whatever works. *Lo que funcione.*

At this point, it must be obvious. I'd been presented with a negotiator's doomsday scenario: a high-stakes, high-tension *no-win situation.* On one hand, I could embrace my friendship with Bill Clinton, endorse his wife for president...and compromise my beliefs. Or I could endorse Senator Obama, honor what felt right to me . . . and lose my most powerful political ally and one of my closest friends.

I hope you're never presented with such a situation, but this is the real world and these things happen. Ultimately, you'll have to choose. It will be painful. It'll force you to negotiate with yourself on a deep level—an ongoing theme in this book, as you'll see. It'll put your character to the test. But I do think you'll know very early on which choice to make, even though you'll lie to yourself about that. Finally, I made mine.

A month later, at a huge rally in Oregon, I endorsed Barack Obama. And it's fair to say: *All hell broke loose.*

Bill Clinton sent out all the attack dogs and some of the more aggressive cats to accuse me of lacking any moral character. James Carville went on national television for the mere purpose of calling me a traitor. "An act of betrayal," he said. "Mr. Richardson's endorsement came right around the anniversary of the day when Judas sold out for thirty pieces of silver, so I think the timing is appropriate, if ironic." For years after, Clinton himself would tell anyone willing to listen, "I'm mad at only two people: Ted Kennedy and Bill Richardson. And Ted's dead." Lucky me—I had the sole claim to Bill's rage.

I had violated the Clinton *omertà*. While once Clinton had felt my pain, now he wanted to inflict it.

I announced my decision at a raucous and, I have to say, thrilling event in Portland. I think I surprised a few people when I arrived; I had regrown my beard after dropping out of the race, during what I called "a period of decompression." The rest helped; my speech was as highly charged and joyful as any I've given, and just as well received. I praised Senator Obama as "an extraordinary American." I pointed out the merits of his "historic speech" earlier in the week, in which he had addressed the controversy surrounding his outspoken pastor, Jeremiah Wright, and the issue of race—an issue important to me for obvious reasons—"with the eloquence and sincerity and optimism we have come to expect of him." Most important, perhaps, was that "he spoke to us as adults." I pointed out that Barack "could have given a safer speech. He is, after all, well ahead in the delegates count for our party's nomination." I hoped that this raw fact—Barack had the nomination sewn up—might be enough to explain why I hadn't endorsed Hillary; it was time for our party to come together. After all, I was the sixty-second superdelegate to weigh in on his side, compared to just five for Hillary. Yet I felt I should say something extra to try to smooth over the relationship with the Clintons as much as possible. "Now, my great affection and admiration for Senator Clinton and President Clinton"—no reason not to lay it on thick at this point, I had nothing to lose—"will never waver. . . . The 1990s were a decade of prosperity and peace because of the competent and enlightened leadership of the Clinton administration."

Then the pivot.

"But it is now time for a new generation of leadership to lead America forward."

Hearing it again now, I understood why it stung. I was painting the Clintons as relics of the last decade. They had built that bridge to the twenty-first century, but now we were eight years in. I was saying it was high time for someone else to drive over it.

I couldn't stop thinking about tomorrow.

I should have left it there, enough damage done. But after the rally, I also said to the assembled press a few things about what I saw as the caustic tenor of Senator Clinton's campaign in recent weeks—comments that probably didn't help my case with the Clintons. Nothing too controversial: "I believe the campaign has gotten too negative." But let's just say if Bill wanted to inflict a mortal wound, Hillary probably would have finished me off.

Before the general election, I tried to make amends directly with Hillary, hosting two fund-raisers for her to help defray her campaign debt. I can only assume she appreciated the gesture, at least; she certainly took the money.

More recently, she asked me to advise on Egypt issues as that country struggles with its post–Hosni Mubarak transition. I was flattered by the request and took it as a sign that there might be a thaw in the relationship. I told her I'd be happy to help, but that to work together effectively we had to dismiss the tensions that had built up over the years. I also told her I needed her to smooth things over with her husband. *They were a team*, after all—a lesson I had learned the hard way. I needed both to agree that we were resetting the relationship. I followed it up with an e-mail directly to Bill: "Let's bury the hatchet."

Bill never responded.

Over the years, I've offered a figurative olive branch at least four times, in direct e-mails and even a thoughtful letter or two. Unfortunately, they went unanswered; I never got any positive response from someone I had known for over two decades. So, when I was asked at the Democratic National Convention in 2012 how I would characterize my relationship with Bill, I had to admit there wasn't one. As much as it pained me to say it at the end of a long friendship, "I have to assume the breach is permanent."

I have come to recognize that this is largely my fault. Although I suggest that I deserved better than the silent treatment, the fact that Bill Clinton felt angry enough to give it to me means that I hurt him.

I maintain that it's not the fact I endorsed Obama that was our undoing; to some degree, that's merely politics. Plus, I meant what I said about the Democratic Party being at a crossroads—we needed to rally behind the future of the party. No, my error was much more tactical than that, and it began and ended back in Santa Fe. I didn't just disappoint Bill Clinton when he came to watch the Super Bowl with me; I embarrassed him. By letting him attempt such a photo op, I exposed him to the possibility that he would fail, and fail publicly. He wanted to come, and I let him. He invited the cameras, and I let them in. He put his reputation for getting what he wants on the line, and I let him hang there.

That's not what friends do.

Yes, at times, you even have to negotiate with friends. They may want something you're not willing to give up. They may even assume you will give up the goods simply because the friendship exists—*friends do anything for friends* and all that. But I simply was not candid with my friend from the outset. If anything, friends owe friends complete honesty. Sure, if I had said, "I'm sorry, Bill, but I can't give you what you want on this one" before he ever boarded a plane for New Mexico, he would still have been angry. Maybe we'd still be on the outs. But then again, maybe not.

Damn rookie mistakes.

So then, is the breach permanent? I assume it is, but who knows: Maybe it depends on the definition of *is*. Although I fear it doesn't.

North Korea:

HANG ON TO YOUR HATS

BY THE TIME I WAS GAPING at my own reflection in a sixty-inch flat-screen ultra-HD television while wearing the latest high-tech 3-D glasses and a silly grin—in a country with little electricity to spare, let alone to spend on the latest immersive display technologies—I knew that this trip wasn't going as I had planned.

It's always a victory to merely arrive in North Korea.

It is, quite simply, the most secretive country in the world. I never take a visit for granted, and I'm grateful simply for the experience of stepping off the plane at the Pyongyang airport, aware that few foreigners, and even fewer Westerners, and even fewer Americans, have such an opportunity. This trip was no different. We went to North Korea to try to persuade the government to stop their missile launches and underground nuclear testing. Additionally, I wanted Eric Schmidt of Google to talk to them about the virtues of the Internet.

I was also there on behalf of Kenneth Bae, a forty-four-year-old Korean American from Washington State who had been detained by the North Korean government for six weeks. I had hoped to be escorting him quickly back to the airport; instead I was taking a virtual stroll, alone, around a computer-enhanced, real-time rendering of downtown Pyongyang as it might look in springtime. That it was a glacially slow stroll—even I could tell that North Korean computing power left something to be desired—only added to my growing frustration.

I had to admit, the diplomatic side of our efforts thus far on this trip had been, well, a bit tripped up. We knew it would be tricky. We had arrived only a few weeks after North Korea, defying the will of the world, had made another dramatic attempt to launch a long-range rocket capable of delivering a nuclear warhead. After a few apparent (and apparently embarrassing) failures, this time the launch had succeeded. The liftoff delighted the nation's young leader, Kim Jong-un—the Supreme Leader's childlike joy while watching the event was played on a loop on state television during our entire stay—but dismayed the world community. North Korea insisted it was a peaceful test for future satellite deployment, merely proof of their new strength and unerring commitment to *Juche,* the official state ideology of *self-reliance* invented by their departed "Great Leader," Kim Il-sung. The rest of the globe, notably the countries within shooting distance, worried it was an intentionally provocative test of ballistic missile technology intended for nuclear weapons. At the least, it was "a product demonstration," as former senator Jim DeMint described it, for Iran and other countries "that want to see if these things work, because we know North Korea wants to sell them." Whatever it was, it violated about a hundred United Nations resolutions. When we arrived, we didn't know what we were in for. The only clear signal was that North Korea was in a rebellious mood.

Nor were we even remotely certain why Bae, who'd been operating tours of North Korea for tourists, had been detained. The official North Korean news agency report certainly wasn't very helpful: Its headline declared merely that there had been an "American Arrested For Committing Crime," and that those unspecified crimes were "proven through evidence."

Your honor, I must object.

That's not exactly a fair trial.

Other reports suggested Bae had been caught with a hard disk filled with sensitive North Korean documents. One theory, just as plausible, was that Bae's arrest was merely to collect a bargaining chip to force the United States into talks over nuclear and other issues.

Maybe so—perhaps they thought the United States would take notice. But the United States wasn't there. I was. And as is my wont, I was eager to talk—to even the world's most secretive country on the heels of the world's most provocative nuclear act. My commitment to the premise that in negotiations it is almost always better to talk than to stonewall—in other words, it's better *to actually negotiate*—is why I had come on this private humanitarian mission, and why I had brought with me Eric Schmidt. Eric, after all, is not only the executive chairman of Google, but also perhaps one of the most prominent advocates of the merits of open communication. He's built a very successful company around that position. If you don't believe me, just Google him.

But as I took a virtual walk through Pyongyang, I admitted to myself that although our trip was not a bust by any measure, neither could I call it a grand success. At least not yet. The simple fact that we had been granted access to the Korea Computer Center (KCC) was an unexpected victory. Few Westerners had been allowed to poke around in this building, which operates as something between a consumer electronics show and a computer lab for postgraduate engineering students. The latest North Korean computer innovations are on display, even though they're unfinished and the country's most promising techies continue to tinker with them.

Permission to enter was something of a coup, especially for Eric, who had come with me to North Korea to deliver a message of greater online access and, even more specifically, increased mobile phone adoption. He was tempted by the opportunity to preach the Gospel of the Internet, believing as he does that an unfettered connection to the outside world is an imperative step for any developing country, even one like North Korea that had spent the last few decades falling off the developed world.

As he told Jang Chol, the president of North Korea's National Academy of Science, "That's my religion, and I'm sticking to it." (Although during our four days here, his sermons were hardly asking to move heaven and earth: "Put simply, I'd like you to turn the Internet on," he told Jang, and any other North Korean scientist who would listen.) It was also a coup for the engineering students to host Eric; they clearly revere the chairman of one of the reasons to hope that their computers not only stay on— the power goes out somewhat regularly here, as it did twice during our visit—but also might one day be connected to the Internet.

The KCC, even the walk through virtual Pyongyang, was a refreshing change. Earlier in the day our small delegation had been given a highly choreographed tour of the E-Library at Kim Il-sung University, a modern facility that, despite a hundred humming computers, stays colder than a butcher's freezer. Miraculously, the cold didn't seem to bother the students there. Truth is, nothing seemed to bother them. Even as our delegation was trailed by a dozen clicking cameras and reporters, the students behind the terminals were utterly unfazed. We were a walking, talking, buzzing, rolling distraction, a swarm of wool coat–wearing bees invading their workspace, yet they didn't so much as lift their heads to determine what all the fuss was about. It was hard not to conclude that they had been directed before our arrival to keep their noses in their terminals, to act the part of computer students engaged in the act of being computer students. In short, to pretend.

But their directors got a few things wrong: First, almost no students were actually *typing* anything; they just sat expressionless, reading documents on a preloaded screen. It was too clean. Too neat and tidy. The fraudulence was inescapable, and unnerving.

"It's like a Potemkin classroom," one of our delegates whispered to another between camera clicks.

It was also worth asking to what degree those terminals were even connected to the outside world. When we were afforded an opportunity to chat with a couple of the students— although under enough supervision that, honestly, we felt bad putting these students in the spotlight, lest they say something out of step with Workers' Party credo—it became clear that what the students referred to as "the Internet" was more often than not merely the *intranet*—the Internet once it had been downloaded, scrubbed, filtered, and reposted according to the demands of the North Korean government. In Google terms, the filter settings were "SafeSearch: Very Much On."

The Korea Computer Center, however, was something different. There were, apparently, secrets lurking. When one member of our delegation excused himself to go to the bathroom, all hell broke loose as two of our minders—they always travel in pairs, so they can mind each other as well—rushed down the hall after him to make sure he wasn't entering any restricted rooms. Hard to say what they were worried about. Perhaps they thought he'd find the Internet ON switch. Or maybe he'd discover the room where they were keeping all the heat.

Our visit to the KCC was a consolation prize—an intriguing one, and tantalizing for a techie like Eric, but a consolation prize nonetheless—provided to us by the Foreign Ministry in the hope that it might soften the blow as the accomplishment of the other two of our three goals faded away: to meet with the American detainee and secure his release, and to meet with Kim Jong-un on a range of matters. The fact that we were being afforded at least a hearing for our third goal—to urge the notoriously clamped-down regime to crack a window to the outside by turning on the Internet for more than the privileged few—was a cornerstone victory.

There were other consolations, too, and they were similarly diverting. We attended a performance of the immensely talented North Korean acrobatic team, whose flying feats put Cirque du Soleil to shame. Even in the near-freezing auditorium, the tiny North Korean men and tinier North Korean women twisted and turned in triple flips a hundred feet in the air. It was doubly impressive that they did it all without a net. ("And without an Internet," someone said. Probably Eric.) Later, our minders took great pride in showing us their "American-style" fast-food restaurant—no doubt under the mistaken assumption that we are proud of our *own* "American-style" fast-food restaurants. The replica was impressive but imperfect; here, too, they got some important things wrong, starting with the ingredients. I half-expected Ronald McDonald to pop up from behind the counter and ask if I'd "like rice with that?"

But: One more day down.

As our dreams of meeting with the Respected Leader ticked away, the Foreign Ministry made us an unspoken bargain: *We'll trade you the Respected Leader for one Great Leader and one Dear Leader.* That is, while they stalled on the answer of whether they'd arrange a meeting for us with Kim Jong-un, as yet another consolation they offered us a visit to the Kumsusan Memorial Palace of the Sun, where the bodies of Kim Il-sung and Kim Jong-il have been given the full Madame Tussauds treatment and lie in state for occasional public viewing. For the time being, we had no choice but to accept. So we climbed back into the vehicles we had been loaned for the week—a caravan of three white SUVs of slightly different makes and models, which cut quite the stark profile as we drove from our Foreign Ministry guest house toward town through the snowbanked streets along the frozen river. Throughout our stay, the streets were eerily empty of traffic. Instead, the hundreds of North Koreans we passed were walking miles on foot or pedaling bicycles alone, in pairs, in groups of five. But to what exactly? Their jobs? Their homes?

When we'd first landed in Pyongyang, we were told that we were the first American delegation to visit North Korea since Kim Jong-il's death in late 2011, which is indeed an honor. We were certainly the only Westerners to visit the Palace of the Sun that day, when it was closed to tourists of any stripe. Which is not to say we were alone. Although the parking lot was empty, the mausoleum was packed with thousands of North Korean soldiers and military police officers who had made the long pilgrimage from their home districts to pay their respects to the fallen leaders.

We were escorted past a group of at least one hundred soldiers waiting in line to go through security. Though polite, they seemed to eye us suspiciously—*how come they get to jump the line?* Soon we *all* had to wait in line for what was a very modern moving walkway, surprising less in its modernity than in its sheer length—at least three football fields.

"It's like the world's longest Disney people mover," one member of our delegation whispered.

"Yeah, bringing you right into YesterdayLand," quipped another.

But this was all part of the experience, with its own rules to boot—no pictures, no talking, and no walking. The purpose of the moving walkway, we soon learned, is not simply to move you from point A to point B, but rather to give you the time to appreciate the scenery as you inch by. Here was an endless parade of portraits of Kim Il-sung and Kim Jong-il doing what North Korean propaganda insists its leaders do best: visiting humble North Koreans hard at work in the fields, overseeing the latest North Korean scientific breakthroughs, and providing the famous "on-the-spot guidance" they could somehow muster at will. Like the time Kim Jong-il visited a goat farm and the Korean Central News Agency reported as fact that "Kim Jong-il's on-site instructions and his warm benevolence are bringing about a great advance in goat breeding and output of dairy products."

There's Kim Il-sung standing behind a gynecologist's table—as if he had invented it.

Here's Kim Jong-il pointing at a red tractor—as if he had designed it.

Marvel, great and dear visitor, at the Great and Dear Leaders as they teach the most accomplished North Korean astrophysicists a thing or two about rocket science.

Gaze upon father and son as they soak up the love and adoration of a rice field full of well-fed children.

The portraits comprise an endless montage of propaganda dreams: *If you frame it, they will believe.* By the end of the tour, even a hardened capitalist is eager to see such comically accomplished men in the flesh. But the architects of the Palace have learned how to delay gratification. First comes the trophy room, a cavernous, marble-laden testament to Kim Il-sung's feats of scholarship and general aptitude, filled to the brim with accolades, certificates, honorary degrees, plaques, and plaudits awarded to the Great Leader by foreign leaders and universities around the world. It's overwhelming. One almost expects to see Rosebud peeking out from under a steamer trunk, or the Ark of the Covenant, as gifted by Professor Indiana Jones. A wider look reveals that the vast majority of the gifts were bequeathed by the world's most troubled and unstable countries; it's a cavalcade of failed states. A closer look at the sole gift from the United States—an honorary degree from Kensington University in Glendale, California—confirms the slim pickings of American gifts, and why you have never heard of Kensington University, even if you've been to Glendale. (For the record, Kensington U. was convicted of fraud in 1996 for being nothing more than a diploma mill housed entirely in the law offices of a man named Alfred Calabro. It then relocated to Hawaii, where it was shut down again. Good thing Kim Il-sung never made it to Texas; it is illegal to use a degree from Kensington University in the Lone Star State. Seriously.)

A short walk, and soon we were in the train station. Well, not an entire station, but a room with Kim Il-sung's private locomotive, pulled to a stop inside the Memorial Palace. It's parked there so visitors can have a peek inside the very train car that took the Great Leader as far as West Africa on a lifelong whistle-stop tour of fellow authoritarian regimes. For its time, it's nicely adorned. Kim may not have had a 747 at his beck and call, but Train Force One appears to be a classy substitute.

After the trophy room, and the train car, there's the waterfall. Or at least it sounded like a waterfall. Or was that applause? What was that noise? As we turned the corner, we discovered the source: a series of chambers that blast jets of air, which as we walked by ostensibly decontaminated us of whatever parasites or foul odors or who knows what we might have brought in with us.

Heaven forbid we infect the Great Leader, considering his poor state of health.

But the next room was the reason for the pilgrimage, the sanctum sanctorum of socialism, the walk-in crypt of the Great Leader himself. A quick left and, suddenly, there he was: Kim Il-sung, lying in state but looking no less animated than the day he debuted his gynecologist's table. I think it an odd choice to bathe the room in a red light, as they have—it added what I have to assume was an unintended haunted house vibe. We were led in by military police, who prompted us to follow their lead: a bow at his feet, a bow at his right side, a walk around his head, and another bow at his left side.

We did not bow. They didn't seem to mind.

Then the entire process—precisely the same rooms, same dimensions, same train car, same eerie red light—was repeated again on a different floor, this time for Kim Jong-il. Or as one member of our delegation put it, after succumbing to gallows humor: "Second hearse, same as the first." There were three notable differences: In the Dear Leader's train car, the notepad on the Grand Marshal's desk was replaced by a Macbook Pro. (Even from ten feet away, Eric quickly carbon-dated it circa 2010.) One-upping his father, Kim Jong-il had his own private boat on grand display to complement his private train. And finally, there was a second ceremonial gift from the United States to add to his own honorary degree from Kensington U., prominently displayed in his replica trophy room: a commemorative coin from the inauguration of our forty-second president, William Jefferson Clinton.

But who are we to judge whether he deserved such accolades? After all, this is a man who, according to Korean state media, reportedly invented the hamburger, wrote more than a thousand books while a college student, and shot eleven holes-in-one the very first time he ever tried his hand at golf. Kensington University should be proud.

It was all very fascinating. A rare experience. Unique and unforgettable.

And probably leaves you wondering—*What does all this have to do with negotiation?*

Everything. Understand my state of mind as I walked through all these North Korean sites. *I was here on business.* I was here to try to rescue an American detainee. The North Korean government knew it all too well. So while it may have been an honor to visit the leaders' final resting place, this entire scenario illustrated one of the classic tactics from Negotiation 101: stalling.

It was clear that our handlers were keeping us at a firm distance for a variety of reasons: to test our patience, to delay possible concession making on their end, to remind us that we were their guests and under their control, to exercise power, as one-upmanship, you name it. As a negotiator, the real test for me is whether or not I want to be patient. As a negotiator, I have to decide for myself what they see from me (for I was being observed this entire time, of course). As a negotiator, I have to have power over their power.

For now, that meant tolerating their propaganda tour. The real game would start soon. I was able to handle this entire process smoothly because this is how the government here operates, and I'd been negotiating in this country for a long time. . . .

North Korea is where it all started, this negotiating-with-thugs business. I owe my moonlighting gig in hostage rescue to North Korea—or as the North Korean government prefers to call it, the Democratic People's Republic of Korea, even though it isn't democratic, isn't a republic, and has had a notoriously fractured relationship with its own people. If it weren't for the DPRK, I wouldn't have begun my two-decade career going face-to-face and toe-to-toe with the world's despots and dictators in the hope of fostering peace, negotiating consensus, and occasionally rescuing an American or two.

The crazy thing is, it began by accident. You could say I was in the wrong place at the wrong time. In 1994, less than two months after President Bill Clinton signed what was being called a "framework agreement" with the DPRK intended to effectively dismantle North Korea's nuclear facilities and therefore, as he put it, "make the United States, the Korean peninsula, and the world safer," I was on a flight to North Korea to see just how much safer the world was truly becoming. We had first landed in Beijing as part of a congressional delegation—a *codel*, in Washington-speak—although on this particular trip I was the only congressman. The itinerary was packed; we were due to visit China, both Koreas, and a few other stops. Though I admit it was North Korea I cared about most, if only out of sheer curiosity. We'd have a full thirty-six

hours on the ground in Pyongyang at a time when few foreigners were allowed any at all, and we'd be there at a time when
North Korea was facing a reckoning. Its *songun,* or Stalinist
military-first culture, and the collapse of its trade economy
with Russia after the Cold War, meant that food production
had stalled, and its citizens were starving. This dynamic
quickly became a vicious cycle, stalling not only economic
growth, but average physical growth as well: Starving North
Koreans grew to be two inches shorter than the citizens of
South Korea—with whom they were still technically at war—and
before too long the North Korean military was forced to lower its
height requirement for enlistees by an inch. The government
would allow its citizens to suffer, but not the size—in numbers,
anyhow—of its army. (Today this relatively small country—
geographically, it's approximately the size of Pennsylvania—has
the fourth-largest military in the world.) The growing chasm
between north and south didn't stop there; even now, it is said
that the economic disparity between North and South Korea
is quadruple the size of the disparity between East and West
Germany when it reunified in 1990.

North Korea has always had an antagonistic, often incom-
prehensible relationship with the outside world, even with its
supposed allies and friends. Perhaps the most comical example: More than once, when its ally China transported food aid
via train to Pyongyang—an obvious gesture of goodwill if
there ever was one—North Korea kept both the aid *and* the
trains, apparently insisting that the trains were part of the aid
package. The befuddled Chinese train engineers had to return
to China by other means. Some were forced to walk.

By the time I first arrived in 1994, many North Koreans
were losing faith in a government that had failed to deliver on
the socialist paradise it had promised. Between the end of the

Korean War and '94, only a few hundred citizens had defected. A few years later, in 2001, the estimated number had grown to a few hundred *thousand*. The official newspaper of the Korean Workers' Party, *Rodong Sinmun*, thought it could motivate citizens to rededicate themselves to their country by reminding them of Kim Il-sung's against-all-odds battle as a guerrilla fighting Korea's Japanese colonial rulers in the 1930s and 1940s in what became known as the Arduous March. Now, it implied, was this generation's time to march on to the future despite the growing odds and obstacles.

They asked too much; it was hard to march under an official government proclamation that citizens only "eat two meals a day." By some accounts, one out of every ten North Koreans would die of malnutrition in the next four years.

But as we boarded the flight into Pyongyang, we didn't know just how bad things were getting. Frankly, we didn't know much at all. Despite its other failures, the country had succeeded marvelously in shielding itself from prying eyes, and its citizens from the outside world. Cold, hard facts were hard to come by. Intel was guesswork. The view from afar was much like today's satellite maps of the country at night: North Korea had gone dark.

That darkness was both figurative and literal, by the way. Pyongyang airport is shockingly dark, especially in light of its servicing a major city. Flights are few—largely because only non-Koreans are allowed to leave, so planes arrive both infrequently and half-full—and electricity is used sparingly. I barely remember runway lights. Landing in darkness in Pyongyang has always felt to me a bit like I imagine landing on Mars must feel.

The flight takes less than two hours between Beijing and Pyongyang, but the trip takes its passengers back fifty years. The difference between the two airports—true in 1994 and

2013—defines the word *stark*. Both serve the largest cities in two flagships of communism and socialism, but the Beijing airport is a modern marvel, while the airport in Pyongyang is essentially a warehouse. It is bathed in fluorescent lights reflected by gray walls. Even the requisite portraits of Kim Il-sung and Kim Jong-il, impossible to miss in the arrivals terminal, look drab. The effect is transporting: You sense not only that you've stepped back into the fifties, but also that it comes only in black and white.

When we passed through customs—really just a uniformed man with a clipboard—the darkness ended. As soon as we stepped outside into the subzero chill, lights powered on everywhere. Click, click, flash, flash. Cameras and reporters, dozens of them. I expected a few, but was surprised by the number. We were blinded, and honestly, I was a little flattered. All this attention, for just little old me? Fair enough; I knew there'd be some curiosity about my visit. But my plan to answer a few softball questions about my straightforward diplomatic agenda was thwarted when a reporter from Xinhua, the Chinese news agency, put his microphone in my face and revealed the real reason so many had gathered—and taught me an object lesson about being prepared for anything.

"Mr. Congressman! Mr. Congressman! What can you say about the American helicopter?"

I had no idea what he was talking about.

"The helicopter. Shot down. Inside the DPRK."

I hadn't heard a thing about any American helicopter being shot down anywhere. Neither had any of my staff. Suddenly I was the one with the questions. But before I could muster even one, the North Korean official assigned to us stepped between me and the cameras. He hastily motioned that the interview was over and urged me to the waiting car.

On the drive to our guest house, I demanded some answers. Deputy foreign minister Song Ho-gyong confirmed that an American helicopter had been shot down after flying over the demilitarized zone into North Korean airspace, and that two Americans from the "enemy helicopter" had been taken into custody. When he tried to change the subject, I didn't let him. In fact, I told him that my mission in North Korea had just changed: I wouldn't be leaving without the army pilots. "It is critically important," I told him, "to turn over these pilots to US authorities." He shrugged me off, saying it was the military's prerogative, and we would have to wait until they completed their investigation of the crash; as an official in the Foreign Ministry, he could do nothing.

As a consolation—the first of many I'd receive during my trips to North Korea—he reminded me that the ministry had scheduled a dinner in my honor once we arrived at the guest house. I told him I wasn't sure the guest of honor would be there; I had to call Washington. Sure enough, when I finally reached Warren Christopher, the secretary of state, who thankfully had compiled more information than I had, my hunch was confirmed. I wasn't to leave North Korea until I got our pilots out. At least now I knew their names: David Hilemon and Bobby Hall, both army chief warrant officers.

When I finally arrived at the dinner, an hour late, I knew it wasn't going to go well for either my hosts or their "honored guest." They wanted to raise a toast. I wanted to raise hell. Despite the finely appointed banquet they had arranged, I told them that there was only one item on the table from here on out—the safe return of the Americans. It was a classic stonewall: Their hands were tied, they said, until the "investigation" was over.

The next day, I met for eight hours with the chairman of the North Korean equivalent of Congress, the chairman of the socialist Korean Workers' Party, and the North Korean economics minister. Each wanted to discuss some element of the framework agreement, but I was a broken record: "We will discuss nothing until you release these American pilots to my custody." I must have said it a hundred different ways to a dozen different people—so nothing would be lost in translation—but I was getting nowhere.

It was only when I was granted a meeting with foreign minister Kim Yong-nam that I began to see the underlying problem. When even he insisted that the Korean People's Army had to finish up this vague "investigation" before the Foreign Ministry could deal, I realized the real power dynamic I had stepped into. It was the ministry, which seemed possibly willing to talk, versus the military, which wasn't talking—except to accuse the pilots of being spies. So the Foreign Ministry was only stonewalling because they were being stonewalled. In a sense, the ministers' hands *were* tied—in a "military first" country, the military came first.

Songun lived on.

It was a classic problem in negotiation. I was negotiating with the wrong people. I was being asked to settle for "no" from people who couldn't say yes.

If I expected any change in the answer, I had to stop the cycle.

I doubted that I'd be granted an audience with the military, but I wasn't about to back down. So I did the only thing I could do: I upped the ante. I made a new demand, pulling a move reminiscent of an alien arriving on Earth: *Take me to your leader.*

I demanded an audience with Kim Jong-il.

I knew it was a long shot. Kim hadn't been seen, in the Western media at least, since his father's death. Everyone was pessimistic. I was told by the North Koreans that he was still mourning the loss of his father and therefore wouldn't see me. I was told by analysts back in the United States that he was suffering from an acute liver disease of some sort—and therefore wouldn't see me. No one was quite sure if he was even still in command of his country, but one thing was certain: *He wouldn't see me.* It was entirely possible that Kim, a huge fan of American movies, was simply holed up in a screening room enjoying the latest bootlegged film. (Westerns were his favorite.) He wouldn't see me, but I kept asking. And just in case—before I even knew I'd be demanding to go head-to-head with the Dear Leader—I brought along a peace pipe I'd brought with me: a VHS tape of the movie *Maverick.*

The North Korean government might not respond to me, but it might to Mel Gibson.

Things with the ministers went from bad to worse (Mel had nothing to do with it). During our next meeting, not only did Foreign Minister Kim shut down the idea of meeting with the leader once again, he accused me of being an agent of South Korea, intent upon souring relations between North Korea and the United States. When I refused to attend a special performance of North Korean children singing and dancing for my entertainment—hardly an appropriate way to spend my afternoon while American pilots were still being detained—Deputy Foreign Minister Song almost left me in the parking lot. And when I adamantly rejected the idea of going to the airport at the appointed time of my departure, he angrily told me, "Fine, then you'd better be prepared to stay for weeks!" I was, and I told him as much, but the absurd thought occurred to me: While I was stuck trying to rescue the pilots, who would come to rescue *me?*

Desperation always courts absurdity. There I was, demanding meetings, refusing to get in the car, and repeating myself over and over. It was the diplomatic version of a child's temper tantrum. I was doing everything except stomp my feet. But at that point, if the stomping of feet would have helped, this congressman would have stomped his feet.

When the stakes are high, sometimes the tactics hit rock bottom.

The next day, the absurdity reached new lows. It began with my proposal to take a break in the negotiations for no good reason—a little time to cool off seemed overdue. Like squabbling toddlers, we needed a time-out.

I let my North Korean handlers determine my schedule that morning, thinking it might win me some goodwill. At first they proposed a harmless itinerary. We rode the subway. We shopped in a department store. We visited an archaeological museum. But when we stopped by the huge bronze statue of Kim Il-sung and they prompted me to lay a flower at the Great Leader's feet, I categorically refused. Once again, they almost left me in the parking lot.

Unfortunately, I made the mistake of neglecting to tell the US State Department about my grand plan to take a recess from the negotiations. By the time I reached back out to them, they were convinced I had either defected or been kidnapped. They had even asked the German Embassy to help find me. Overlooking the fact that I had almost started another international incident, I'm still amused by the idea of a bunch of Germans speeding through Pyongyang in their Mercedeses, asking if anyone had seen the foot-stomping congressman from New Mexico. *Achtung! Richardson?!*

So how did we finally break the fever? We didn't. Song had spent the day—between his flashes of anger—talking some sense into the military. Though he didn't say it directly, I got the feeling that even the military brass were beginning to see that this whole affair—a humble congressman from New Mexico, patriotically planting his feet in North Korean soil and vowing not to leave until he could rescue his fellow Americans—wasn't playing well for them in the world media. It was David versus the Goliath that was the million-strong Korean People's Army, and David was winning the PR war.

That's a good lesson right there: If you have the high ground in the public eye—whether that public is the actual public or a smaller group of observers invested in the outcome—the pressure on the folks across the table can be enormous, and you don't even have to do anything except enjoy the benefits. It happens in your favor as a matter of course, and it's powerful.

I could see this pressure working some magic. But before Song could relate any good news, he shared the bad: One of the pilots had died in the crash.

Later, we learned the details of the operation, code-named Razorback 19. Chief warrant officers Bobby Hall and David Hilemon had taken off in their OH-58 scout helicopter on the morning of December 17. The plan was to familiarize Hilemon, who hadn't flown in the area, with the contours of the demilitarized zone. Instead, they accidentally flew five miles into North Korean airspace. When a surface-to-air missile exploded nearby, it shattered the canopy and caused an engine malfunction. Hall and Hilemon attempted an emergency auto-rotation maneuver, in which the engine is shut off but the rotors keep spinning. It didn't help; the pilots were flying blind anyhow. Hilemon, of Clarksville, Tennessee, perished during the crash landing.

My mission shifted from rescuing both pilots to making

certain that Hilemon's remains were treated respectfully and returned to American custody immediately. Sensing the gravity of the situation, even the stonewalling North Koreans couldn't keep up the blockade. During our next meeting, Song made an offer. I could bring Hilemon's remains across the DMZ into South Korea—as long as I left along with them. What's more, he hinted, the other pilot would be released "very soon."

Not good enough, I told him. I would need both Hilemon's remains immediately *and* a guarantee that Hall would be released by Christmas, four days later. Even this demand made me a little uneasy; after a week of stomping my feet, I wasn't inclined to depart without Hall—to "leave a man behind," as they say in the military. But after consulting on the phone with US military authorities in Seoul, I was assured that such a guarantee from the North Koreans would suffice. So the next day—after a short, absurd delay when we were told to pay a surprisingly exorbitant hotel bill of $10,000—we crossed the DMZ into Panmunjom and I presided over a solemn ceremony in which the coffin containing the remains of David Hilemon were covered with a United Nations flag.

Christmas came. Christmas went. And as of December 26, Hall was still detained. Since my departure, North Korea had moved the goalposts, now insisting that the United States first "admit its responsibility as the offender" before it would release Hall, newly deemed a "criminal" and a spy. We would later learn they had also dictated a statement they forced him to sign admitting "that this criminal action is inexcusable and unpardonable." Despite having the forced confession they desired, it took another visit—this time by Thomas Hubbard, the deputy assistant secretary of state—to not-so-gently remind North Korea of its obligation to release its captive.

His message: Call him a spy if you insist, but send him home. Even then, only when Hubbard—not Hall—also signed a statement expressing "sincere regret for this incident"— not quite an apology but something that seemed to appease the Foreign Ministry—did they finally release the second American pilot.

Hall landed in Tampa, Florida, at 11:15 p.m. on December 31. He had missed Christmas, but he made it home in time to ring in the New Year surrounded by his family, with forty-five minutes to spare. A few days later, I met up with him for the first time at MacDill Air Force Base in Tampa. He told me he was convinced that the pressure I had put on the North Koreans with my stubborn refusal to leave the country had saved him from being tortured or starved, or worse. I was glad to hear it. Sometimes in a negotiation, progress is hard to discern. So I must admit, learning firsthand that I helped an American reunite with his family is one of those good feelings that don't subside in a hurry.

Perhaps that's why I didn't hesitate when I heard, two years later, that another American was in trouble.

In August of 1996, a twenty-six-year-old Alaskan missionary named Evan Hunziker had been captured by North Korean farmers, turned over to the local authorities, and was being charged with—you guessed it—espionage. If the claims that Hunziker was a spy were true, it's fair to say he had a unique way of concealing his identity: When the farmers discovered him, he was drunk, naked, and swimming across the Yalu River with nothing but a vague idea that he could, as he put it later, "promote peace."

It was a time of high drama in North Korea—it was about to enter major food and energy shortages, and had rattled its sabers on the war front by sending one of its submarines into South Korean waters. But although the North Koreans were therefore touchy about any further international incidents, it appeared at first that not even they believed their own press on Hunziker. As the incident got attention in the media, my contacts in Pyongyang signaled early on that if I were to apply for a visa to come negotiate his release, it would be approved quickly. Even they saw that this captive was no Aldrich Ames; he was simply a troubled young man on a misguided mission. As I put it at the time, "Let's just say he tried to be a little too much of a tourist."

Still, when I arrived in November, this time as an official envoy of the Clinton administration, it became clear the North Koreans weren't going to make it smooth sailing. Despite their earlier cooperation in granting my visa, as soon as we sidled up to the negotiating table, they hunkered down. Even on what should have been easy concessions, they wouldn't budge. Perhaps they thought they could make a play for a few carrots they suspected I'd brought with me, or that a delay would strengthen their hand—I'd like to tell myself they just wanted to enjoy my winning company as long as they could. Whatever the reason, I hit a wall.

I've learned in negotiations that when there's an early stalemate, sometimes the best option is to throw a verbal grenade of sorts to shock the negotiators into starting over. Blow things up, as it were. On this occasion, when the North Koreans wouldn't even answer a question as simple as "Is he healthy?"—

a nice way of asking if they'd been torturing him—I had no choice. I pulled the pin and tossed a bomb they couldn't help but notice.

"Can you at least tell me whether he still has his fingernails?"

I let the intentionally provocative question hang in the air—no smile, no further explanation. It was a risk, and I waited with some apprehension as the interpreter dutifully translated my attempt at bone-dry wit. Would my hosts be offended? Humor is always subjective, especially when so much can be lost in translation.

Thankfully, the North Koreans responded just as I had hoped: After a moment's hesitation, my cohort across the table let out a booming laugh that reverberated among the ministry officials in the conference room.

There's a rule of thumb in public speaking that has become a platitude: Open with a joke. The idea is simple—if you get 'em laughing, you've already won 'em over, and they'll be more inclined to agree with whatever you say next. It happens to be true. In my experience, even a high-intensity negotiation can use a little levity to set the mood, or even more usefully, to warm up a cold freeze. It's a gamble, but in this case you've got the house odds on your side. If it becomes clear early that you're willing to risk a joke, and they're willing to laugh at one, then you're far more likely to come to an agreement. Together, you've recognized the absurdity of what you're doing—in this case, debating over a conference room table the fate of a fellow human being—which is its own kind of bond.

On that day, we didn't know if Hunziker's life was in jeopardy. Later we learned he had, in fact, been threatened with execution. So when I made my joke, I truly didn't know if Hunziker was fit as a fiddle or at death's door. But sometimes the best way to resolve a matter of life and death is not to treat it like it's a matter of life and death.

After the laughter died down, I sussed out pretty quickly their gambit—they wanted money. Fair enough, but their demand for $100,000—ostensibly a fine for Hunziker's trespassing into the country, but more accurately described as a ransom—didn't fly with me. Official American policy is that we don't pay ransoms, for the very real reason that doing so would create a moral hazard: Some things aren't a question of money. Plus, if you pay a little now, you'll pay even more later. Then again, money talks. So soon we agreed on a more reasonable five grand, which we expeditiously called a "hotel fee" for Hunziker's lengthy house arrest. (Although I doubt he ordered much room service.) On November 27, Evan Hunziker was released to my custody.

I'd like to say it was a happy ending all around, but unfortunately freedom wasn't a good fit for Hunziker. On the flight back to the Yokota Air Base in Tokyo, he appeared disoriented and detached from reality—so much so that I took care not to make him available to the dozens of cameras that had gathered for a press conference when we landed. Back in his home state, he faced six misdemeanor convictions and a restraining order from a close friend of his former wife. "He knew that if he went to Alaska," his father said, "as soon as he got off the plane the authorities would throw him in jail." Naturally, he didn't want to trade one jail for another.

Unfortunately, the path he chose was far worse.

Just before Christmas, in a hotel room in Tacoma, Washington, he shot himself with a .357 Magnum.

The world wanted him rescued. We rescued him. But he couldn't save himself.

How sad it is that sometimes it is easier for two sworn

enemy nations to come to terms than it is to save a single life from self-destruction.

I've been on eight trips into North Korea, some for humanitarian missions, others to bring people home to their families. I'm most proud of bringing home the remains of seven soldiers from the Korean War. I'd gone to North Korea as an envoy of the Bush administration in 2007. I hoped that a gesture like that on the part of the DPRK would improve relations. It never happened.

In 2010, my last year as governor, I went to Pyongyang to try to calm the waters between the North and South, as they were on the verge of serious hostilities. The story was covered by Wolf Blitzer of CNN, who was along on the trip. I urged the North Korean regime to stay cool in a very tense atmosphere, and I do think my visit contributed to the North Koreans standing down and showing what I thought was remarkable restraint.

None of these trips has ever been easy sledding. Something is always bound to go sideways. On one trip to get answers about the fates of American troops still missing in action from the Korean War, my friend Calvin Humphrey was introduced to our North Korean counterparts, accurately, as the senior Democratic counsel on the House Intelligence Committee. The translator was sloppy in his translation, and suddenly the North Koreans in the room were livid. It took another translator to determine why. Calvin had been introduced as a "spy."

It's for moments such as these that my associate Tony Namkung, who often travels with me to the DPRK, always brings with him the same trusty hat. "It's my North Korea hat," he says. "That way, when we're about to land for our great adventure in Pyongyang and I tell everybody, 'Hang on to your hats!' I have a hat of my own to hang on to!"

His point is well taken: In the DPRK, you simply never know what you're in for. Certainly, on this latest adventure with Eric Schmidt, I couldn't have known that instead of meeting with the Leader I'd be staring at the lifeless bodies of his father and grandfather, surrounded by bowing North Korean military officers.

The only thing you can count on to any degree in North Korea is the weather. And in January 2013, even as we toured the Palace of the Sun—the irony of the name was lost on no one—it was *cold*. And not merely to keep the bodies of the former leaders on ice.

It is difficult to describe how pervasive the cold in North Korea was during this latest visit. Outside, it was far below freezing, hovering near ten below Fahrenheit. And huddling inside hadn't provided much relief. There is simply no precedent for indoor heating in North Korea. The country can't afford it, and the North Koreans we'd encountered were not only acclimated to the cold, they seemed not to notice, or think it strange, that they were bundled up indoors too.

I hadn't taken off my scarf for days, even indoors—a fashion choice that apparently caught the attention of the outside world. After I returned home, I discovered that a blog had been devoted to it: *Bill Richardson Wore a Scarf During Every Second of His North Korea Trip*. It joined the pantheon of prominent North Korea photo blogs, including *Kim Jong-il Looking at Things* and *Things That Make Kim Jong-il Smile and Frown*. I was honored. Maybe a degree from Kensington University would be next.

Perhaps most telling of the impact of the cold: Our VIP hosts had begun most of our meetings apologizing for it. Even though they have become used to it, they know well enough that foreigners aren't. I doubt this is a cunning negotiating tactic on their part, to keep us distracted and shivering. While their lack of indoor heating helped our argument about their social predicament—they desperately need to improve their economy so that they might one day find ways to afford creature comforts of the twenty-first century—it certainly didn't help us *make* our argument. It's hard to break the ice when the room is subzero. In any event, through chattering teeth we assured them each time that there was no need to apologize to us. (We stopped short of pointing out that the apology they owed was to their citizens, who didn't have enough electricity to heat their homes.)

But I still wanted to do whatever I could to warm things up. We only had one more day scheduled in North Korea. If we were to meet the Supreme Leader Kim Jong-un, or to make any headway on our other negotiation points—the release of Bae, and some assurance that the North Korean military wouldn't continue its nuclear testing—it had to be soon.

Our next—and last—scheduled negotiation session with the deputy foreign minister and the country's chief nuclear negotiator was to be held in one of Pyongyang's nicer restaurants. It began as others had: with an apology for the cold, and a pro forma recitation of the litany of the grand successes that their "Respected Leader," Kim Jong-un, had fostered in the short time he'd been in charge. "Although one year is not a long time," began vice foreign minister Ri Yong-ho, "in that time the trust in our leader has been strengthened beyond imagination."

Beyond imagination, indeed.

"You are all wearing your coats, because it is cold. But even in this cold, surely you can see the many ways that our Respected Leader has improved our country."

Not exactly, but I'm sure you'll tell us.

"He has brought political stability. He has refocused on our economy. And he has presided over a successful launch of a rocket for our satellites."

Yeah, we saw that. Though we may take issue with your suggestion that it's merely for satellites.

Clearly, even in this, our last scheduled meeting, there would be no concessions—or apologies—for their recent missile test. Now that they had missile capability equal to their self-image, there'd be no more need for one. They felt they had leveled the playing field.

But in this meeting, Ri went a step further.

"So yes, I would like to say we can work together. I would like to introduce you to the Respected Leader. I would like to do all of this, because of one reason: I like you, Mr. Richardson."

I'm glad to hear that.

"But it is unfortunate," he continued, looking down into his bowl of noodles, "that the Americans have chosen to antagonize the DPRK with your provocative actions and posture of war. Your country is very hostile to us."

Aha.

I had come to expect this closing statement, and knew to overlook it. It has been the recurring theme in North Korean propaganda over the decades—designed to control its citizens through fear of imminent attack from Americans—and I didn't expect it to subside during our visit. It's as pervasive as the cold.

Still, it often surprises me how matter-of-fact the delivery is. Even the coffee table magazine left to welcome us at our guest house made sure to remind us we had come from a land of evildoers. The closing article was a screed on the subject of the United States—or rather, the "Disturber and Wrecker of the

Peace . . . hell-bent on starting a new war in Korea . . . the main culprit in undermining peace and stability." As an official welcome, that's a fine how-do-you-do.

Of course, one of the reasons I had hoped to meet with the leader was described in that same anti-US screed: "Dialogue is incompatible with confrontation, and peace with war." I wanted to increase the dialogue, and thought that a meeting with the leader would be the most prominent way to do that. Also, I hoped that meeting with Kim would foster our other goals, for both obvious and nonobvious reasons.

For starters, while we were there, Kim Jong-un celebrated his thirty-first birthday. (Or perhaps it was his twenty-ninth, or his thirtieth. We couldn't know for certain, since there is no definitive account of the Respected Leader's age.) Regardless, we were quietly hoping that the Respected Leader might release Bae to our custody if only to celebrate his birthday. His father, Kim Jong-il, would often celebrate his birthday by giving amnesty, and therefore freedom, to thousands of low-level North Korean prisoners, in rare (at most, annual) displays of mercy. Perhaps, we thought, it might be a case of like father, like son.

We had also joked amongst ourselves that perhaps Kim Jong-un might still be feeling magnanimous from his designation, just more than a month prior, as the "Sexiest Man Alive for 2012"—an honorific bestowed by no less a paper of record than *The Onion*, the satirical American news source. It was a piece of breaking satire that the Chinese Communist Party mouthpiece, *People's Daily*, eager to heap praise on its totalitarian neighbor, reported as glowing fact. (One might have thought the Korean Central News Agency would have been the one to take the bait. After all, earlier that year, the "Great Vituperator," as it has been nicknamed for its absurd bombast about us "imperialist Yankee bastards," had outdone itself, reporting the existence of unicorns—specifically, that "scientists" had "rediscovered" the birthplace of the unicorn ridden by the founding father of ancient Korea, which *happened* to be in Pyongyang, which *happened* to further legitimize the current government. Some things you can't make up.)

Anyhow, we surmised, surely the "sexiest man alive" would have no use for a prisoner. After all, what could possibly make a sexy man even sexier than proving he's merciful?

Of course, the primary development we pegged our hopes on was the Leader's very own words—given in a rare New Year's speech just a few days before our arrival, the one that was looped on state media—insisting that he was eager to transform his military-first country into one that put the economy first, "to that of an economic giant in the new century, thus realizing the wish of the great General who devoted all his life to making our people well off with nothing to envy in the world." And in fact, "like the satellite scientists who conquered outer space, we should wage a dynamic campaign to push back the frontiers of science and technology so as to develop the country's overall science and technology to the world standards as soon as possible."

To that end, I hoped that bringing Eric along just might be the ace up my sleeve. As I described him in most of our negotiations, "He may not be our head of state, but he's an *economic* head of state." This is a country that once kidnapped South Korean movie directors to please the whims of its cinemaphile leader Kim Jong-il. Wouldn't Kim Jong-un want to meet Mr. Google?

And in that last meeting, I laid these all on the table.

"Why not? What have you got to lose?" I asked Minister Ri.

He paused, and cracked a small smile.

"I like you, Bill Richardson," he said again.

With a response like that, I knew this could go either way.

"Then why can't we work together on this?" I asked.

And he told me. They had tiptoed around it in earlier meetings, but now they were prepared to put their foot squarely down. "We cannot work together on this because," he said matter-of-factly, "your own government doesn't want you here."

Oh yeah, I probably should have mentioned that.

He was right. Our own government didn't want us there. We had come to North Korea despite a reprimand from the US Department of State. When asked about our trip at her daily press briefing only days before our departure, State Department spokesperson Victoria Nuland said, "We are obviously aware of the trip. . . . Frankly, we don't think the timing of this is particularly helpful, and they're well aware of our views." She said it in about a half-dozen different ways, and then repeated much the same twice more in the days to follow. I was miffed; I felt I should be trusted, as I had toiled for so many years as a member of President Clinton's cabinet and proven my diplomatic bona fides a hundred times over in dozens of countries as a negotiator and ambassador to the UN—North Korea most of all. What's more, I had already postponed the trip once at State's request that I wait until after the South Korean presidential elections played out. I was a dutiful soldier.

But the fact remained: With the reprimand from State, suddenly the negotiations with my North Korean counterparts got that much harder. No longer were Minister Ri and I talking to each other alone, nor was our delegation speaking directly with our hosts. Now there were many negotiators, and one of them—the United States Department of State—wasn't even in the room. They hadn't made the long trip, but now they were the biggest presence.

So I grant that the reprimand irked me just a bit, because it ran contrary to my one guiding principle: It is almost *always* a better idea to talk, even with our enemies. A cold shoulder does nothing but deepen the freeze. Even with the recent missile test, I knew that talking was better than shunning, so I'm not certain why the State Department felt they should undermine a trip that was all-systems-go. Given my choice not to endorse her candidacy for president in 2008, who knows: It's possible that Secretary of State Hillary Clinton, who was about to retire from the position to make way for Senator John Kerry, decided to give me one last kick in the behind before she headed out the door.

If so, it worked. Without the sanction or support of the State Department, it was clear: This time, I brought the wrong hat. As our dinner wound down, so did our prospects. The North Koreans weren't willing to deal. Their most official explanation: "If we give you what you want, that will upset your State Department, since they told you not to come."

Now, I'm not so narcissistic as to deny that what was bad news for our delegation might be good news for our nations. The North Koreans saw that a new State Department was gearing up—this one to be headed by Senator John Kerry—and the DPRK wanted to give that new relationship a chance. Conceding to the demands of one private citizen, Bill Richardson, might send a message that the DPRK didn't value the authority of the Department of State.

Upon our return to the United States, I was happy to report this both publicly—in the *Washington Post*, I wrote that it was "time for a reboot with North Korea"—and privately—in an email to the US deputy secretary of state, I urged that "there seems to be a window of positive engagement with the DPRK." I meant it.

Sadly, that particular window closed. Within a few weeks of our return, the UN Security Council announced yet another resolution, supported by the United States, condemning North Korea's missile test and enforcing new sanctions. And in predictable response, North Korea announced plans for a new round of missile tests, this time "aimed" at the United States. So much for the question of whether the missile test was, as they had insisted to my face, "for satellites, nothing more." This time they were hardly coy. The official statement from North Korea's National Defense Commission was chilling: "We do not hide that a variety of satellites and long-range rockets which will be launched by the DPRK one after another and a nuclear test of higher level which will be carried out by it in the upcoming all-out action, a new phase of the anti-U.S. struggle that has lasted century after century, will target against the U.S., the sworn enemy of the Korean people." If the United States didn't want to talk, neither would North Korea. "Settling accounts with the U.S. needs to be done with force, not with words as it regards jungle law as the rule of its survival."

A few weeks later, they made good on their threat. The North Koreans tested yet another nuclear device, this one smaller than the first two, and therefore more portable—and dangerous—that the North Koreans insist can reach the United States' mainland. They followed that test with even more indecipherable diplomacy: inviting notorious basketball rogue Dennis Rodman and three Harlem Globetrotters to tour the country. (Safe to say, if that group had been able to secure Kenneth Bae's release, I'd have quit the game for good.)

It's hard to know what to make of the North Koreans' actions. But I know this: Next time—and if I can help it, there will be a next time—I'll bring a different hat.

Same scarf, most likely, but a different hat.

Saddam Hussein and the Egyptian Torturer:
IT'S ALL ABOUT THE SHOES

WAS IT SOMETHING I SAID?

I turned to my trusted advisor Calvin Humphrey for help, but he could only shrug. Apparently I wasn't alone; he didn't understand what the hell had just happened either.

We only knew the facts: In the middle of a negotiation to release two American prisoners from an Iraqi prison, President Saddam Hussein, one of the most notorious strongmen ever to grace the planet, had slammed his fist on the table in front of us and stormed out. Of his own conference room. In his own palace. Gone, baby, gone. And I had no idea what I'd done to piss him off.

Hussein is not a man one wants to anger, and we—or someone, or *something*—had angered him. I couldn't see how it might have been something *I* had said, since he had been the last person to speak and I hadn't even done so much as interrupt. In fact, I thought I had been unfailingly polite. Yet the table was still vibrating when he slammed the door behind him. Which meant Calvin and I were now alone, except for a group of our newest closest friends: eight glowering members of the Republican Guard surrounding us and Iraqi foreign minister Tariq Aziz, none of whom offered to help or made any suggestion about what we were now expected to do.

I turned to the most neutral man in the room, my interpreter.

"What the hell is going on?" I asked him.

"You crossed your legs," he said.

"What?"

"You crossed your legs."

"So?" I asked.

"You showed the bottom of your shoe."

"So?!"

"That's an insult in Arab culture."

I wanted to say that storming out of a negotiation without an explanation is an insult in American culture, but I chose not to. (Besides, I had occasionally chosen to use similar tactics myself, as you'll see. Who was I to judge?)

"So what happens now?" I asked.

The interpreter said simply, "You're in trouble."

Tariq Aziz finally spoke up. "You must apologize," he said.

"To who?" I asked. "An empty chair? He *left*, Tariq. What do you expect me to do?"

"Congressman Richardson," he said again, "you must apologize."

I wasn't sure what would happen next. Would the Republican Guard arrest me for wearing a loaded loafer? Would Saddam ever come back? Would Calvin and I be taken hostage as well?

It wasn't one of my best starts in a negotiation.

The beginning of any negotiation is precarious, most especially if the negotiator across the table is known for being unpredictable. He needn't be a murderous dictator—you don't come across one of those every day—but if he's somewhere on the spectrum from occasional hothead to temperamental madman, you have to play it right from the get-go. And speaking immodestly, if there's one vital skill I've refined over the years, it's how to take the measure of a man or woman quickly and determine from the first handshake how best to set the right mood.

Setting mood is an important power gambit early on in a negotiation. If you're successful in setting the tone you want, you've framed the conversation: its intensity, its candidness, its comfort level. If you allow the other party to do this, you'll have to waste time and energy swinging the mood back to where you'd like it to be. That gives you more opportunities to step in something you don't want to.

Oh, and here's the touchy part: An attempt to set the mood is, at best, guesswork, and at worst, gambling. You won't know you've screwed it up until it's too late.

But as much as Saddam Hussein would teach me about hijacking a meeting's tone, I have to say my riskiest gambit on this front was how I once greeted notorious Egyptian army general Omar Suleiman, the right-hand man to Egypt's then-president, Hosni Mubarak. This was in 2007, and as "assistant" despots go, they don't come much more despotic than Suleiman. Egypt has had a spotty human rights record in recent decades, and it's fair to say that Suleiman can take most of the credit. As the country's intelligence director since 1993, Suleiman had been accused of running a systematic and enthusiastic program of torturing political detainees. He was a hands-on guy to boot; he was reputed to perform some of the wet work himself. Supposedly, when the American CIA once asked Suleiman for a DNA sample from a relative of an Al Qaeda leader, he made a better offer: "Why not the whole arm?"

(To be fair, it's also said that he cooperated in the US extraordinary rendition program, a controversial policy used for years after 9/11 that allowed our government to transfer terrorism suspects we wanted interrogated to countries that allow torture. It was known that if we wanted someone worked over, we'd send that someone straight to Suleiman.)

In short, he was a bad guy. Even if he was, at times, *our* bad guy.

The circumstances of my visit were already precarious. At this point in 2007, while I was smack in the middle of my run for president, my savvy foreign policy advisor, Mickey Bergman, suggested I take a detour from the campaign trail and attempt a rescue of Gilad Shalit, a soldier in the Israel Defense Forces who had been abducted by Hamas a year earlier. We thought a prisoner exchange deal might be on the table. But we knew two inconvenient truths: First, that Egypt expected to be the brokers of any such deal, and second, they didn't necessarily want outsiders playing an active role, since they had their own vested interests in any Israeli–Hamas exchange that might take place. As history has shown, pretty much anything to do with Gaza is delicate.

Mickey and I weighed a prickly dilemma. Whom should we approach first, the Israelis or the Egyptians? Mickey pointed out that without Egyptian consent to a deal there would be no deal at all. Approaching them first would show them the respect they expected, and would send a signal that we knew they were partners in the process. But he also explained that if we went to the Israelis first, we would hear straight from the horse's mouth just how serious they were about striking a deal. Armed with that information, we could then go to the Egyptians with solid intel. (Without torturing a soul.) It was decided: Israel first.

We had to do it quietly. If word of my trip reached Egypt, we'd have problems. We invented a cover for the entire trip—we announced publicly that I would merely be seeking economic investment in New Mexico from my Israeli and Egyptian friends. This was legitimate. During these trips, I did indeed take meetings about possible Israeli and Egyptian investments in New Mexico. In fact, I gave an economic speech in Cairo for a group of businessmen, along with my New Mexico economic development secretary, Fred Mondragon. It was a win-win as it allowed the other negotiations to take place.

Our twenty-four hours in Israel went as planned. We met with president Shimon Peres, foreign minister Tzipi Livni, Ami Ayalon of the Knesset, and Gilad Shalit's father. Not surprisingly, all were far more interested in the return of the young Israeli soldier than they were in investing in New Mexico.

Setting up a trip to Egypt—and securing a meeting with President Hosni Mubarak—was a more difficult matter. To do it, I had to go through Omar Suleiman.

Prior to our trip to Israel, I called him directly (miraculously, Mickey had somehow acquired the strongman's personal phone number; this is how valuable your team can be!). I wanted to make a first impression. I also hoped to precook an agreement with Suleiman to meet, and to arrange a meeting with his boss, Mubarak. At first he was reluctant, but over the course of the phone call he warmed to the idea. I could tell he was going to assent soon, and that's when I did something that to this day still amuses me. When he finally agreed to meet—"Yes, I shall greet you when you arrive"—and then moved on to say something else, *I clicked* OFF *on my BlackBerry and put the phone down.*

No kidding. I hung up on one of the world's most notorious strongmen.

I figured I had gotten what I had come for—frankly, the *only* thing I had come for, since I didn't really have much interest in making small talk with a torturer—and I knew that a continued back-and-forth with him could only produce more opportunities for something to go wrong. So yes, *I hung up.*

Sound rude? Deliberately inflammatory? Well, it is a power move, that's for sure. I don't recommend using it if you want to build a long-term relationship. But the man I was dealing with hurt people, deliberately, for his own gain (and amusement, for all I knew). He needed to know that even though we could work together, that was the extent of my interest in knowing him.

Later, when I watched the film *Moneyball*, I smiled when I saw that I'm not the only one who has employed this arguably undiplomatic tactic. In the movie, Oakland Athletics manager Billy Beane is negotiating with the Baltimore Orioles' general manager for a key trade, and when he gets what he wants, he slams the phone down. Peter Brand, as played by Jonah Hill, is perplexed.

"I think he was gonna say something else," Brand offers.

Beane, in the guise of Brad Pitt, explains the tactic in a way I can only agree with: "When you get the answer you're looking for, hang up."

After Israel, it was off to Egypt. We flew into Cairo in the middle of the night, prepared for two important meetings. The first was with President Mubarak, set up by Suleiman. That, too, was fairly uneventful; the president and I talked reasonably about the prisoner exchange deal that might be struck to return Shalit. He confirmed what we had already come to know: "We want the deal to be done." A good sign.

There was just one more stumbling block. You have to understand the power dynamic between Mubarak and Suleiman. Because even though Suleiman had arranged our meeting with Mubarak, I felt it proper that Mubarak bless our upcoming meeting with Suleiman (this is how it works at high levels sometimes). But instead of asking directly, I employed a tactic that works in many negotiations. Don't ask for a yes; assume a yes. Then merely pose it as a fact and see if they object. So: "Mr. President, I'd like to thank you for letting me meet with Omar Suleiman." He merely nodded. The lesson? When they don't object, take it. It's yours.

That impending meeting with Omar Suleiman had our collective blood pressure rising. We had only one club in our bag, and that was to reassure Suleiman, and thereby his boss, Mubarak, that Egypt would get full credit for any prisoner exchange deal.

You might ask, *Why not just reassure Mubarak directly during that first sit-down?* Well, it's that power dynamic I mentioned. Suleiman had his influence. Enough so that he could scuttle the deal if not properly, well, massaged. Basically, we were required to speak with him. So with mere reassurance in hand, we needed to convince Suleiman not to be a spoiler. The only other plan? Schmooze the torturer.

The guy I'd hung up on.

So after our meeting with Mubarak, we piled into a van and headed to—

Well, actually, I wasn't sure.

I turned back to Mickey and asked, "Where to?"

He looked back at me.

"We're headed to a meeting with General Suleiman, the head of Egyptian intel—"

"I know *that*, you idiot." I was laughing. He knew I wasn't calling him an idiot. Or maybe I was.

"But where is he?" I asked. "Where are we going?"

At this point, we were just driving through Egypt aimlessly.

"I thought you'd know," he said.

"I pay *you* to know," I said.

"Well, it's . . . at . . . Suleiman's office," he said sheepishly.

"Yes, but where is *that*?" I demanded.

Mickey could stall no more.

"Well, I assumed we'd just drive around until we ran into a bunch of dungeons and people being tortured. Suleiman's gotta be around there somewhere."

I have to admit, I thought that was very funny. As much fun as it would have been to pull over and ask a stranger "Which way to the dungeons?" we instead contacted the president's staff to help us find our way. And this little conversational detour would prove vital to the negotiation.

When we arrived at the meeting with Suleiman, I knew I had to practice what I've long preached about all negotiations: Set the right tone, and set it early.

Because what we walked into was the wrong mood entirely. Oh, it wasn't a dungeon, per se, but considering the mood I felt needed to be established, it was a bit dangerous: an astoundingly long table suited for ten people a side; notepads and bottles of water carefully placed to set a very formal mood; and, on Suleiman's side, ten glowering men, including the nine staffers Omar had recruited to make him seem all the more intimidating.

The first thing I did was shore up my ranks. I had planned to have only Mickey and Clinton staffer Rob Malley at my side. But that would have meant we were embarrassingly outnumbered. I looked around and quickly told Marcus, an unarmed security guy we had brought along with us from New Mexico, to sit down with us and put on his best I'm-a-diplomat-too face. He was game, and I was grateful. Heck, if a janitor had walked by, I might have recruited him as well.

But that was only half the battle. I knew the other half had to be waged in the minutes that followed. Suleiman began pontificating on the state of affairs and the importance of achieving balance between Israel, Hamas, and Egypt. In other words, he was setting the tone. Which meant we weren't talking about Shalit. We needed to be talking about Shalit.

So about ninety seconds in, I interrupted. That's right, I cut off the man who had probably tortured people for far less.

"General, General, General—" I said. It was obvious he was surprised. "General," I continued, "I'm going to let you go on with your speech in just a second. But I have to ask you something first."

He stared back at me.

"Here's what I need to ask." I looked at Mickey, then back at Omar. "On the way here, I asked Mickey—"

I pointed to Mickey, the terrified-looking Jewish man who had no idea where I was going with this.

"—how we knew where were going. And he said we'd know when we were there because there'd be dungeons, and we'd hear the screams."

Mickey just about fainted, but I charged on.

"But I have to say, Omar, this is nothing like I expected. You have a very nice office!"

Dead silence.

For at least ten seconds (Mickey insists it was more like ten hours), Omar Suleiman just stared at us.

Then he burst into laughter. As did his staffers, once they saw it was permissible to do so. From then on, the tone of the meeting was exactly as casual as I wanted it to be. In fact, I soon suggested to the general, "Why don't you send your people out of the room, and I'll have my people leave, and you and I can discuss the matter candidly." He agreed.

So, in the end, Omar Suleiman didn't torture me. But I have a feeling Mickey Bergman wanted to.

It was a gamble, but it paid off.

It's fair to say that Saddam Hussein taught me how necessary gambling like that can be. As I waited for him to return to that palace meeting in July 1995—my feet now planted firmly on the ground—I contemplated my first big gamble in a high-stakes negotiation. Which was scary at the time, since the president was clearly ticked off at me. Hell, I was ticked at myself—my ignorance of Arab culture had allowed a despot to hijack the meeting's tone. To, in fact, take complete control of the whole damn thing.

Well, I wasn't about to bail. I was there for a reason.

I had been summoned to Baghdad at the behest of Peter Bourne, the former drug czar under President Jimmy Carter. The Iraqis had reached out to me through him to see if I could facilitate the release, to the satisfaction of all parties involved, of two American contractors they had arrested three months earlier. It's hard to believe now, but Iraq had been relatively quiet during that time—four years after the first Gulf War—as sanctions applied by the UN were thought to be successful. Even famous troublemaker Saddam Hussein hadn't been able to make the usual noise that had so often caught the attention of the world community. But on March 13 of that year, Iraq once again nabbed the headlines when Saddam's border guards arrested two American contractors they claimed had crossed into their country illegally. Forty-two-year-old David Daliberti and thirty-nine-year-old William Barloon had been working as oil mechanics for defense contractors in neighboring Kuwait and looking for a UN observation station when they got lost in Iraqi territory. They were arrested and charged with entering Iraq without permission. Even a small offense like that can bring a hefty sentence, and sure enough the men had been sentenced to eight years in the Abu Ghraib prison (yes, *that* Abu Ghraib).

While the Clinton administration did not contest the charge of crossing into the country illegally (the men apparently had had a couple of beers and didn't do the best job of reading their maps), they did press for the return of the men as a humanitarian gesture. That's where I came in. Peter Bourne had told me that both Jimmy Carter and Jesse Jackson had tried to make headway on the matter, but their attempts had stalled; maybe I could restart the process. I was happy to try.

My instructions from the administration were clear: "You're on your own on this. We don't want anybody to hear that you're talking to the Iraqis, because they're our enemy. But we want these two Americans freed. So as long as you stay under the radar, as long as you don't screw up, we're not going to say anything. But if you screw up, if this gets out, we're going to say we know nothing about it."

In the following months I flew regularly to New York to

meet with Iraq's UN ambassador, Nizar Hamdoon. It was a dicey proposition, since I had to keep my motive for these trips very quiet among my compatriots in DC. And as cruel fate would have it, I kept running into our own UN ambassador, Madeleine Albright, in the airport. To this day, I feel bad about the lies I told her to keep at bay her suspicions about why I was truly headed to New York. *I'm giving a speech to a Hispanic group,* I told her. *Uh, I'm off to drum up Wall Street business for New Mexico,* I insisted. I might as well have told her I was headed to a Knicks game. In fact, maybe I did.

Despite the secrecy, I was keeping quiet channels open with the White House, and consulting regularly with national security advisor Tony Lake. He had assigned one of his Middle East experts to help me out, and the pair helped me navigate the rough waters of this particular freelance diplomatic undertaking with one of the world's most unpredictable regimes.

Over a sumptuous Iraqi feast, Hamdoon confirmed that the Iraqi regime had no compelling interest in keeping the men in custody. Still, the ambassador made a dozen demands in exchange for the release of the men, including that President Clinton write a letter formally thanking Saddam for his action. I knew Hamdoon didn't have much of a hand, so I didn't even bother to let him play it.

"Not a chance," I told him.

"It is an imperative," he said.

"Not a chance, Nizar. And if you ask again, I'm leaving."

"Congressman, President Hussein requires—"

And without another word, I got up and left.

Leaving is a bold move in a negotiation—just ask Saddam— but if you have the stronger position, or if you're dealing with someone who is less than the final authority on the other side, you can usually get away with it. *Once.*

It worked. A week later Hamdoon called back and asked to continue our talks. As a consolation, I told him that he'd get nothing from President Clinton, but that if they agreed to let the contractors return with me, I'd make a statement as a United States congressman. He agreed.

It helped that the contractors' wives had run a very strong (and surprisingly successful) international media campaign to embarrass the Iraqi regime into releasing their husbands. The regime was ready to do it. What wasn't clear was whether Saddam himself was ready to see them go. If he had been, certainly President Carter or Jesse Jackson would have had better luck. Even Hamdoon had his doubts. "It will depend on how he feels when he meets you in Baghdad," he said.

Thankfully, after three months and ten meetings with Hamdoon to work out the details and the ground rules, I was on a flight to Baghdad with Calvin. We had one of the most difficult assignments we could comprehend: Head to one of the world's historically hottest hot spots to see if we could bend the world's most inflexible dictator to our will.

Despite the green light, I had a hunch it would be one of my toughest negotiations. I didn't know it would also be one of my strangest.

Before the final leg of our flight to Baghdad, Calvin and I stopped in Amman, Jordan, to meet with US ambassador Wes Egan. We thought it would be a housekeeping visit, but he brought the first bit of unsettling news to the trip. While we had been en route, an Iraqi radio broadcast had alleged that an escape attempt by Barloon and Daliberti had been thwarted the day before. We thought it was bullshit based on the timing of the broadcast. The Iraqis knew I was headed their way to negotiate the release of the men. Where they trying to gain some leverage? Were they setting me up for a fall?

What's more, Egan said he had spoken with the chief of staff at the Jordanian royal palace and that King Hussein bin Talal was under the impression that, contrary to my negotiations with Hamdoon, I was in fact bringing Saddam a formal apology from President Clinton and was speaking on behalf of, and with the full authority of, the United States government. Egan had tried to clarify that no apology from Clinton was forthcoming, and that I was only traveling there as a single congressman, not as an official envoy of the government.

That's a risky spot to be in for a guy who negotiates with so many international powers. Why the danger? Well, the more I insisted to the Iraqis that I was not representing the US government, the more at risk I was of breaking federal law.

Since the last year of the eighteenth century, there has been a law on the books in the United States that specifically prohibits any private citizen, "wherever he may be," from carrying on "any correspondence or intercourse"—in other words, negotiating—"with any foreign government or any officer or agent thereof, with intent to influence the measures or conduct of any foreign government."

This law was passed during the administration of President John Adams after a pacifist named George Logan went rogue and tried to negotiate on his own, directly, with the French government. His goal was sound—he merely wanted to avoid a war with France—and it's said that he was somewhat helpful. Historically, the Logan Act has been more of a threat than a promise. No one has been convicted of violating it. Logan himself was a popular figure, and was even elected US senator from Pennsylvania—thereby making his self-appointed authority official—although try as he might, even in his new state-sponsored capacity he never could repeal the act that bore his name.

My goals were sound, too, but that didn't mean I wasn't treading on thin ice. As far-fetched as it might sound, the fact is that my attempts to get these American contractors out of an Iraqi prison could have landed me in an American one.

The next morning we set out on an exhausting 510-mile drive out of Jordan and through the Iraqi desert. The trip was herky-jerky, at times slowed to a standstill by traffic tie-ups created by merchants selling their wares, at other times speeding well over a hundred miles an hour through the flat desert. Our party transferred to a fresh set of cars several times—as if we were trying to shake off someone on our tail—but we finished the last leg in a black, high-performance Mercedes whose driver had an allergy to the brake pedal. When the road was clear, holy cow. But when the car would overheat or the road was cluttered—with potholes, camels, or discarded remnants of the weapons used in the Gulf War—we'd sputter to almost a standstill, much to our driver's chagrin. The trip took the full day, and while it would be taking too much license to suggest that by the time we reached the Baghdad Sheraton we thought it was a mirage, it's no exaggeration to say that I've never looked so forward to lying down on such a mediocre mattress.

Unfortunately, sleep was not on the agenda. Tariq Aziz, Iraq's foreign minister, wanted to meet right away, even though it was past 10:00 p.m. I knew what they were up to. It wasn't that they were in a hurry; they knew we'd be exhausted from such a long journey, and that would give Saddam an edge in whatever negotiation we were about to have. Dictators around the world have played this game when I've met with them: Castro in Cuba, al-Bashir in Sudan. I must admit I've employed the same tactic: *Get 'em while they're tired.*

The meeting time appeared to be nonnegotiable, so we threw our bags in our rooms and sped to the Foreign Ministry for the negotiation before the negotiation.

It began poorly. Tariq had drafted two documents he expected me to sign before I could meet with Saddam: one, a letter indicating that the Clinton administration appreciated the humane act of releasing two American criminals, and two, a commitment to a second visit to follow up on whatever agreements Saddam and I might make. To buy time, Calvin and I retreated to a separate room and with very little discussion agreed that I couldn't sign either. I was frustrated, to say the least. It was as if those ten meetings with UN ambassador Nizar Hamdoon had never been relayed to his bosses.

It was late. Thankfully, Tariq spoke fluent English—he had studied the language at Baghdad University and worked as a journalist before joining the Baath Party—because if we had had to wait for translation, I'm fairly sure I would have fallen asleep right in front of him. I can only assume it would have caused offense. Despite the hour, however, Tariq spent the next few hours doing what I have come to expect in sessions like this: complaining about the treatment of Iraq at the hands of the United States. I'd offer all the details here—he vented for quite a while—but suffice it to say that he wanted the United States, and the United Nations, to lift their sanctions on the poor, beleaguered, war-torn country that had done no wrong.

I could have argued on that point, but did not.

Finally, after hours of this, Tariq informed us that we'd be meeting with Saddam the next day, and that he was expecting to discuss the release of the two detainees.

"That's good to hear," I said.

"Perhaps," he said.

"Why just *perhaps*?" I asked.

He echoed what Hamdoon had said a few weeks earlier. "It shall depend on how Saddam feels when you speak with him," he said. "My advice to you? Don't make him angry."

In my mind, the Iraqi president was suddenly the Incredible Hulk:

You wouldn't like me when I'm angry. SADDAM SMASH!

Little did I know, right?

Sure enough, the next afternoon we were brought to one of Saddam's many palaces. I've always found palaces that have sprung up from the desert an eerie sight, but this one was even more unusual. Inside, the rooms were as ornate as any I had seen, but they were empty. (Americans would become familiar with the interiors of these palaces, since many were used as headquarters for coalition forces during the Iraq War.) But the most peculiar sight came as we were escorted into the meeting room where we'd have our negotiation with Saddam. It wasn't the decor that amazed; the walls were curtained, perhaps to avoid prying eyes, but they weren't curtained well enough. At the bottom of one, along the wall, just peeking out from the bottom of the curtain, were the toes of a half-dozen shoes.

We weren't alone.

Our best guess was that those wearing them were Saddam's bodyguards—size 9½ wide, by the looks—trying to stay inconspicuous in a room that didn't offer many places to hide. To say the least, it was a strange sight, a stranger tactic, and one of the strangest moments in my entire career in foreign policy. I wondered what it must be like to be one of those men, where it's your whole job to stand alert and protect your president while your face is buried in a curtain. I doubt any Secret Service agents have had to endure a post like that. The whole moment still makes me chuckle. I'd gone toe-to-toe with plenty of despots. But this was the first time I had ever gone toe-to-toe-to-toe-to-toe-to-toe.

That's when Saddam marched in, one of the most notorious, murderous, vicious—

Wait a minute.

It wasn't Saddam. It certainly looked like Saddam, right down to the mustache. But it wasn't Saddam. I considered the possibilities. Was it one of his look-alikes? I had heard about the collection of doppelgangers that Saddam was said to have assembled over the years—rumors more than proved facts— men hired for their resemblance to the Iraqi dictator who could be used as decoys or cannon fodder. Could this be one? And was I supposed to fall for it?

Then another Saddam walked in, this one looking a little less like the original, but still replete with that iconic Saddam mustache. Then, after him, another Saddam. Then another. It was like there was some VW Beetle full of Saddams in the next room. But as less-convincing Saddams entered, I determined that these men were members of the famed Republican Guard, who showed their allegiance in part by grooming themselves accordingly. Imitation isn't the sincerest form of just flattery, but subservience as well. These particular guardsmen were the military officers detailed with protecting Saddam, his traveling bodyguards.

(So who, I had to wonder, were the men wearing the shoes behind the curtain? To this day, I'm still clueless . . . and fascinated.)

Then the real Saddam walked in. Yes, this was the dictator in the flesh.

He was a big man, tall. I don't want to call him handsome, but he had . . . let's call it *presence*. I'm not easily daunted—at least, not anymore—but as he sat down and stared at me with his dark eyes, I admit that I thought to myself, *What the fuck am I doing here?* There was an aura around Saddam Hussein, but a dark one. Of all the dictators and despots with whom I have negotiated, by far Saddam carried with him the most intensity. As my New Mexico deputy Eric Witt reminded me later, I said of Saddam shortly after the meeting, "His eyes are like the eyes of death."

Those were, of course, the eyes that would soon catch sight of the sole of my shoe.

Now I waited. Saddam had stormed out. And I had to rescue the situation. The translator had said to apologize. Foreign Minister Aziz had said to apologize.

And yes, when you offend someone, especially when the offense is based on your ignorance of that person's customs, and in that person's house (or palace, as it were), an apology seems like the right move.

Which is why I said to myself, *You know what? I think he*

expects *an apology. I think he thinks I'm an American weak-ling. So I'm not going to apologize. But I'm going to be respectful and I'll pursue my agenda.*

So we all sat there. I had no way to know how this gamble would pay out, if at all. But apologizing was no guarantee of any progress, just as *not* apologizing offered the same possibility. So it went back to setting the tone. Saddam had hijacked the room by leaving it. I decided to take it back by . . . waiting.

In reality, I had nothing to bargain with. So I manufactured an asset: silence. Or, at least, the hope that strength would be seen in my silence. In my calm and my patience.

When you hear the expression *minutes seemed like hours,* yeah, we were feeling it.

After fifteen minutes, Saddam walked back into the room as if nothing had happened.

I tried to remain poker-faced when I saw him, but inwardly I blew out a huge sigh of relief. We continued our discussion of the release of the two contractors. I did not apologize, and I think he respected that. By now, our meeting was approaching its second hour, and two Americans were counting on me. I cut to the chase. "On behalf of the American people and President Clinton," I said, "I would like to request the release of the two Americans in your custody."

Saddam said nothing.

"If this effort is to succeed, you must begin to trust me," I said.

Still nothing.

He was nonplussed, or at least appeared to be. So I relied on a vital negotiating tactic. I needed to be completely direct about what was in it for him.

"The current relationship between our countries is not helpful for Iraqi citizens or the United States, and it has poten-tially drastic implications for the entire region, including the

Israeli–Palestinian problem. Should you release the two Americans, I believe the American people would appreciate this humanitarian gesture."

And with that, I stopped talking.

It was his turn.

Only he didn't take it. Instead, he just sat there, staring at me, giving me a full dose of those dark eyes. I've learned that dictators are never in a rush to hold a normal conversation. They like to let you stew in your own gravy. These are always uncomfortable moments, when your negotiating partner is either playing games or trying to keep the ball on your side of the court. We often have a tendency to want to fill the silences, if only to relieve the pressure. That can be dangerous. After you've said your piece, any further moves might stick your neck out too far. You might say something you didn't intend to. Next thing you know, you've negotiated against yourself.

So we sat there, in silence. A standoff.

As a man of the American West, I half expected a crow to squawk and a tumbleweed to blow by.

One minute.

Two minutes.

Finally he spoke.

"Based on the principles that you have appealed to me, and on the respect that you have shown me, and the request of Bill Clinton, and the long journey you have taken without any reassurances, I will use the constitutional powers vested in me in the Iraqi constitution and release the two individuals to your custody. You will be able to take them with you."

As the interpreter translated his words, I reached out and grabbed Saddam's arm as a gesture of appreciation. Bad move. All eight of the Republican Guardsmen reached for their guns.

Luckily, Saddam didn't give the order to shoot. What a headline that would have been:

Richardson Negotiates the Release of American Detainees, Dies

Saddam continued to speak, inveighing against the failures of American foreign policy, but to be entirely candid, I wasn't listening. I had gotten the men I'd come for, and I was already imagining the looks on their wives' faces when we got home.

After he finished, Saddam invited the Iraqi state media into the room to snap a few pictures to mark the occasion. As the flashbulbs popped, he leaned in close. "You know, Congressman Richardson," he said, "it doesn't help me in my country to be photographed with you."

I said, "Mr. President, I can assure you it doesn't help me either."

And Saddam Hussein laughed.

That seemed as good an exit line as any, but as I tried to inch my way to the door, Saddam said something I did not see coming. "I understand," he said, "that you want to go to Sunday services."

It's true I had told one of his assistants that I am Catholic, but I don't recall mentioning any Sunday plans. "You are in luck," he said. "Tariq will take you to Mass this afternoon." (As it turned out, Tariq's wife is a Chaldean Catholic.) As reverent as I consider myself, staying for Mass would have violated one of my personal commandments: *When you get what you want, get the hell out* (I'll go into *much* more detail on that tenet later, in another chapter). And we had gotten what we wanted: the release of the two Americans.

"Unfortunately, Mr. President, I must return to America immediately to cast votes in Congress."

He seemed to understand, but still had something to say.

"Very well. But if you go to Mass, don't go to confession."

"Why not, Mr. President?" I asked.

"Because knowing about your career, you're going to be there forever!"

And we both laughed together. I can't say I liked the man or was sad to see him leave the world years later. But we had worked together. We had talked. We had made a connection. We had respected each other. And we had set two innocent men free to return to their wives, and their lives. So we did something good.

As we left the room, I glanced down. The six shoes were still at the bottom of the curtain.

What was *up* with that?

––––––––––––––––––––

"I'm Congressman Bill Richardson from New Mexico," I said, "and you've been released to me. I'm taking you home." We were in the Polish embassy, where the transfer had been arranged, and when Daliberti and Barloon heard those words, they both started crying.

"Are we in trouble?" Daliberti asked me.

"No, you're heroes," I reassured both of them.

Hearing that made the tears fall even more freely.

Later that night at the Sheraton, we popped open some champagne and we ate pizza. Calvin toasted the men and poured liberally from a bottle of good Scotch. It was, to say the least, an emotional scene.

When my phone rang, I pretended to be surprised, but I knew precisely who was on the other end. President Clinton had, of course, taken a keen interest in this international incident, and he was anxious to see it have a happy ending (he even mentioned it in his memoir). I spoke to him briefly. "Billy, you did it," he said. "Bring them to the Oval Office when you come home."

"I will, Mr. President."

Then I handed over the phone to the men.

"It's for you," I told them, and both men took a turn receiving the praise and thanks of the president of the United States.

I had my own meeting with the president upon our return. His curiosity was typically Clintonian.

"So: Saddam. What's he like?"

"He's everything you imagine," I told him. "Street-smart. Strong. Unpredictable."

"Is he someone we can deal with?"

"No," I replied. "I don't think you can ever make a deal with the guy. He'll try to intimidate you. He certainly tried to intimidate me."

"How?"

I told him how Saddam had stormed out. I told him about the huge entourage of Republican Guardsmen.

But I never told him about the shoes.

Sudan:

GET IN, GET ON WITH IT, GET OUT

GET THE VICTORY AND GO.

If there's one thing I've learned over the decades in my negotiations in almost every time zone, it's that minutes matter. In a negotiation, no matter how big or small, no matter how domestic or international, at home or away, the smartest move you can make is not only to take yes for an answer—which is an important first step—but to take that yes as far away as possible as quickly as possible, before the person who gave it to you can even think to take it back.

Get the victory and *go.*

Strike the agreement, run for the border.

I learned this lesson—or at least, it has been reinforced a few times over—in a rather unlikely place. Africa, as a rule, moves slowly. Try to do something in a hurry in Africa, and the land itself has a way of saying, *Whoa, not so fast.* Continental drift, after all, was invented here—so to speak—and it seems to have kept its copyright. Any visitor to the continent can get caught up in its inertia. What should take hours can take days. What should take days takes weeks. What should take a few months might never happen.

This is, of course, part of Africa's great appeal. I've personally found my time in Africa extraordinarily valuable, because its sheer size, and its glacial pace, force a new perspective on you. It's a continent of grand vistas and long sunsets. Of endless prairies and three-week safaris. Of half a dozen time zones, each unspooling in real time. It makes you take stock.

Tune in to a National Geographic Channel documentary and you'll see the few minutes when Africa is a flurry of activity—the tiger racing after a wildebeest, or a dik-dik bounding over a bush—but it rarely shows you the other twenty-three and a half hours, when the entire continent is lazing under a baobab tree. Tomorrow the lion will race across the grassland, sure, but the lion sleeps tonight.

Yet the country of Sudan, while in the heart of Africa—if Africa were a human body, Sudan is approximately where its heart would beat—is no place you'd want to slow down. Routinely ranked as one of the most dangerous countries in the world, it is the largest nation in Africa, but one of the globe's poorest. Its political instability—and the opportunity for mischief such instability permits—has perennially earned it a spot on the United States' list of state sponsors of terror. Never mind cotton and sesame; for the last decade, as perhaps more than a million Sudanese civilians were slaughtered in the Darfur region at the hands of the Sudanese government and the Janjaweed militias, Sudan's main export has been violence.

Which is why, as much as I adore the continent of Africa, the country of Sudan more than frays at my nerves. It has me eyeing the exits. But as I say, it has also taught me a vital lesson about negotiation, which I'm happy to repeat.

Get the victory and go.

Get in, get on with it, get out. When you hear yes, ideally the next sound you hear should be either the conference room door closing behind you or, in my case, propellers quickly spinning up for the hasty flight out of the country.

In 2006, I was summoned to Sudan when forty-four-year-old Paul Salopek, a prizewinning reporter for the *Chicago Tribune*, had been arrested and jailed for being a spy.

As a reporter, it's fair to say that Salopek was, and still is, something of a rebel. Between stints as a scallop fisherman in Massachusetts, he began his career in journalism—and his association with my home state of New Mexico—in 1985, when his motorcycle broke down on a ride through the city of Roswell, in the southeastern part of the state. To afford the repairs on his beloved bike, he took a job reporting on police affairs for the local paper. It may have been an inauspicious start to a career, but journalism quickly became a calling, and led to a career covering Central America, New Guinea, and the Balkans. He thrived on the job; just more than a decade after taking a newspaper gig merely to pay off his repair bills, he won a Pulitzer Prize for reporting on the Human Genome Diversity Project. Three years after that, he won another, for his work in Africa—namely, for covering the epidemics of diseases and the political turmoil rampant in the Democratic Republic of the Congo. When the Pulitzer committee granted Salopek the award, it made special mention of the fact that in order to cover even the most war-torn region, he would often travel by canoe.

So he may be a rebel—a free spirit who travels by trusty canoe and unreliable motorcycle—but he is a rebel with a cause: illuminating the strife in deep Africa. Shining a light on what's been called the Dark Continent.

Winning two Pulitzers, it turns out, doesn't mean much to Sudanese rebels. In the summer of 2006, when Salopek took a leave of absence from the *Tribune* and returned to Africa on a freelance assignment for *National Geographic*—to report on the Sahel, the zone of biological diversity where the land transitions between the northern Sahara desert and the plains of Sudan—his trip earned him a different kind of notice. Upon slipping across the border from Chad, he was detained by rebels sympathetic to the government—many of them children armed with automatic weapons—and threatened with execution. Only with some fast talking did he convince his captors to hand him over to the Sudanese military, a group only slightly more reasonable. They didn't release him; on the contrary, he was charged with entering Sudan without a visa, with reporting "false news," and, of course, with the granddaddy of international misunderstandings: espionage.

Not long after, his wife, Linda, wrote me a letter requesting my help. I accepted.

This would not be the first time I ventured to Sudan. A decade earlier, in 1996, while in my eighth and final term as a congressman, I landed in Khartoum with a similar goal: to talk a rebel leader by the name of Kerubino Kwanyin Bol into releasing three Red Cross workers, including fifty-one-year-old John Early, an American pilot from Albuquerque. (To this day, I'm still not sure what makes my fellow New Mexicans so eager to travel to Sudan just to get into trouble!) The trio had been taken captive after landing at the wrong airport at the wrong time—Wunrock, in a barren and remote part of southern Sudan. Worse, they carried with them an unfortunate cargo: five wounded fighters loyal to another rebel leader named John Garang, Kerubino's lifelong rival for power within the Sudan People's Liberation Army. Wounded or not, they were the enemy, and the Red Cross workers were their ride. Well-meaning or not, in a violent hothouse like Sudan, it's fair to say they were more than pressing their luck. They were asking for trouble.

Although Osama bin Laden was no longer in Sudan—the government had sent him packing to Afghanistan a few months before, in response to pressure from the United States and Saudi Arabia—Sudan hadn't exactly improved its international rep. The country was still complicit in a number of terrorist plots, and the United States had even taken the extreme measure of transplanting its embassy from Khartoum to Kenya. In other words, so worried was the United States about its embassy workers in Sudan that it would rather see them based in Nairobi—hardly a secure position, and where, as cruel fate would have it just two years later, the United States embassy *was* bombed, killing hundreds. Madness.

Even though they both opposed the Sudanese government, the blood was bad between Kerubino and Garang. At first, the prospects for freeing the Red Cross workers, who had already been in captivity for five weeks when we arrived, seemed even worse. I wasn't sure if Kerubino was a rational negotiator. I had been briefed by the International Committee of the Red

Cross that he was impetuous, had trouble concentrating, and couldn't focus on one subject for more than a few minutes. (Such an attention span is perhaps why, although he claimed to be a Christian, he also claimed to have eleven wives.) Whereas Garang was American-educated and -trained—at Grinnell College and Iowa State University in Iowa and Fort Benning in Georgia—Kerubino was essentially uneducated. I didn't know if he would respond to pure reason. I feared he might not budge.

Landing at a remote airstrip in southern Sudan—our pilot buzzed the ground once to check for rocks and potholes—didn't exactly provide a foundation of confidence. Nor did being surrounded by preteen boys with AK-47s as we made our way to the small village and the smaller chieftain's hut where I was to meet with Kerubino, surrounded by roaming goats and wildebeests.

What's more, what I had been told about Kerubino's lack of focus proved spot-on. He rarely concentrated on the reason for my visit, choosing instead to launch into a series of unconnected diatribes about the oppressive US sanctions on Sudan.

In the end, though, the negotiation seemed like a lopsided success for our side: Kerubino had begun by demanding $100 million in ransom money, but with some arm-twisting on my end, he settled for far less—what the *New York Times* accurately reported as merely "five tons of rice, four Jeeps, nine radios and . . . a health survey for their disease-ridden camp."

Lopsided, right? I really took him for a ride, right?

Not even close, and here's a good lesson in negotiation. A closer investigation of that last deal point—the health survey— reveals its real value, and why I felt it would be welcome when I proposed it. As we entered the village, I had noticed—it was impossible *not* to notice—that children were falling prey to disease and malnutrition left and right in Kerubino's rebel camp. I soon learned that Kerubino's own daughter had died of measles only two days before our meeting. One of Kerubino's sons, just four years old, was dying. The health of his own family was *the* elephant in the room—even amid the few actual elephants not too far away—and I felt it had to be addressed. So I made my appeal to Kerubino personal, suspecting that he might respond more to emotion than to reason.

I asked to see his son.

He didn't have to be asked twice. We headed to the ramshackle hospital tent and visited his son, who was lying on a cot amid other sick children. I'm no doctor, but even I could see his son *was* dying.

We returned to the hut, and after five hours of negotiating, I finally leveled with the man behind the men holding the machine guns: "Listen, I can't deliver the money," I told him. "But look around you. You don't need money. You need aid. I can get you aid. You can help your children, and the children of your village. I can help you do that. Look at the water you're drinking. It's dirty. It's making your people sick. It's making your own family sick."

He was listening.

"You don't have clean water," I told him. "But you do have the power to save your children, and to save the future of your people." I offered him a survey team that would assess the water quality and then implement necessary improvements, and he saw the wisdom in my words. He hadn't received his $100 million, but I suspect—I hope—that he felt we struck a fair deal.

A lesson for all you despotic tyrants out there: Even a vicious warlord can have the right priorities.

And a lesson for you negotiators, too: Don't presume that what's valuable in your world is of equal value in someone else's. Once you understand what another person values—really, truly values—your next move often becomes obvious. In this case, water was more valuable than gold.

Taking my own advice, I didn't wait long after Kerubino assented to our agreement to hop a flight out of the country—a quick meal of the aforementioned goat, a firm handshake, and soon I was headed to Geneva for a hasty press conference, where I stated the obvious: "It was a totally surreal atmosphere." Then we hopped a flight back to DC in advance of the press conference where Bill Daley fainted—and where the president, in announcing my appointment as US ambassador to the United Nations, noted with bemusement that I had eaten goat in a chieftain's hut only days before.

Now, ten years later in 2006, I hoped to repeat the relatively quick, clean success with the release of the journalist Salopek.

Get the victory and go.

Prior to the trip, I had been contacted by the Sudanese ambassador to the United States, Khidir Haroun Ahmed, in what I thought at first was just a call from an old friend to rekindle a relationship. "You may not remember me," he admitted, "but we met when you rescued those Red Cross workers a decade ago. I was a personal aide to President al-Bashir back then. Do you remember?"

To be honest, I wasn't sure if I remembered. In my haste to rescue the hostages back in 1996—to get in, get on with it, and get out—I hadn't taken close notice of names. It was a blur of goats and goatherds, heat and handshakes. And yet this man seemed sincere. So I dispatched my aide, Calvin Humphrey, to find out when and how Haroun and I might have first met. After some reconnaissance, Calvin said the story checked out: Sure enough, Haroun had worked as a translator as Kerubino and I worked on a deal to release the Red Cross workers. And now he was Sudan's ambassador to the United States.

So when I received the letter from Paul's wife, Linda, asking for my help in releasing her husband, I knew to check in first with Ambassador Haroun. I figured that he would know—if anyone could know—if I had a chance of getting the speedy release of Salopek.

We were in luck. The ambassador not only was willing to help, but also held me in high regard, grateful that when I had secured the release of the Red Cross workers back in 1996, I'd been careful to thank the government of Sudan for its assistance. Giving credit to the government, at least, was a gesture of goodwill that was good enough for him.

There are two lessons in negotiation right there, the first of which is often put crudely: "The asses you kick on the way up may be the asses you kiss on the way down." Or, put in more diplomatic terms: Be diplomatic to everyone, even if they aren't yet diplomats. And the second is when you strike a deal, do your best to make sure everyone feels good about it afterward—which includes giving the other parties credit for their help in getting things done. People remember how you treat them.

As a result, Haroun—pardon me, *Ambassador* Haroun— was also eager to butter me up. Even among African ambassadors, the scuttlebutt was that I was going to run for president in the next election. Which meant that I would be spending time in the caucus and primary states, and Haroun wanted to make sure he was on my radar, for a reason I had never anticipated: Apparently there is a sizable Sudanese expat community in Iowa. *Who knew?*

Clearly, Ambassador Haroun would be an ally in our effort to release Salopek. I went to visit him at the embassy in DC, and I asked him if he could give me any assurance that this story might have a happy ending. If I was going to get involved, I wanted to precook this release to the extent possible. So I laid it out for him: "Ambassador, we need to get this guy out. And frankly, *you* need to get this guy out. You're getting terrible press over this, and for good reason. He *is* a journalist. He's not a spy. On top of all your troubles, you don't want to be the country that journalists around the world are giving bad press to because one of their own is behind bars."

Then I leveled with him: "Tell your president that his friend Bill Richardson wants to come get this guy out. And tell him that if he lets this guy out, this time I'll say nice things about the president, too. Not just the government."

And just to make it personal: "Plus, I'll tell the State Department that *you* were the key guy here."

This, he seemed to understand.

When we met for dinner a few days later, the ambassador began by giving me an update on Sudanese–American relations. "I've talked to the president, and as you know, he has some complaints about America."

Yes, I did know. The world knew.

"He has some complaints about America, but—"

But?

"But he is very fond of you!"

Oh great—just what I needed. *Bill Richardson: Every*

African Despot's Favorite Politician. That's not exactly the press I wanted as the 2008 election approached.

"Whatever you do," I told the ambassador, "don't let that get out!"

He didn't get my joke. Instead, I went back to the business at hand.

I told him, "Look, I want this to happen. I want to take a plane, and I want to go help release this man." Ambassador Haroun seemed encouraging, but still a little noncommittal. I realized he couldn't make a direct promise, but I looked him square in the eye: "If you were me," I said, leaning in, "would *you* get a plane?"

A few days later, after he made a few well-placed calls to a few well-placed countrymen, the ambassador only had to say a few well-chosen words to let me know that the prospects looked good:

"Get a plane."

Several high-profile US officials had visited Salopek in jail before me, and although they hadn't yet negotiated his release, they and others had weighed in on the subject of his unacceptable detention. Christopher Shays, the United States senator from Connecticut, flew to Sudan with US ambassador Cameron Hume, and after the pair met with Salopek, Shays asked for forgiveness on Salopek's behalf: "Paul did a very foolish thing coming into the country without a visa," he said. "He knows that. He knows he made a mistake." Senator Shays then asked for a sense of perspective. "But it's not in anybody's interest—in their or our government's—to have this blown out of proportion. This is a reporter doing what reporters do."

Others made similar appeals. Speaker of the House Dennis Hastert. Jesse Jackson. Even Bono of U2 called for Salopek's release. The rebel journalist had become an official cause célèbre. Perhaps the most notable official who tried to visit Salopek in jail was a first-term United States senator. Barack Obama had been on a fact-finding trip to Kenya and intended to make a stop in Sudan. Unfortunately, he wasn't granted a visa. He wasn't about to repeat Salopek's mistake of coming anyway; thankfully, that didn't stop Senator Obama from granting an interview. "From all indications," he said, "this guy is a wonderful reporter. He's done terrific work." Senator Obama then called on his home country to act. "This is unacceptable and I expect the U.S. government to take this with the utmost seriousness."

At the very least, even if Obama and the others hadn't made it to Salopek's jail cell, I hoped they had softened the ground before me. I was looking to make this quick.

To get in, get the victory, and go.

Then again, *Africa* has its way.

Whoa. Not so fast.

If something was going to go wrong—if our best-laid plains would somehow unravel—it was going to go wrong in Africa.

Ha. Who am I kidding? You don't need Africa to screw things up.

I did indeed get my plane—a beautiful G4, which a friend offered as a humanitarian gesture. Unfortunately, the pilot didn't seem so devoted. When he heard our destination—Darfur, in the heart of Sudan—he balked. "Darfur? But that's in a terrorist country," he protested. I couldn't entirely disagree. I could only point out the value of our mission, and that a fellow

American was counting on us. I added the fact that we still had an ambassador assigned to the country, and an embassy operating there. He seemed to care about the well-being of Salopek, but the embassy argument didn't seem to sway him. "Not good enough," he said.

"Bullshit. You're flying this plane."

He seemed to appreciate my determination—I like to think he could see the steel in my eyes, right?—and before too long we were taxiing down the runway.

Soon we leveled off and cruised. And then:

"Um, Governor?" asked Albert, my security guy.

"Yes?"

"Do you have your passport?"

"No, I don't. You have it. You have all of them."

"I don't have any of them."

"You were supposed to have all of them."

"I don't have yours. I don't have mine. That's why I asked. Calvin was in charge of the passports."

I turned to Calvin, my aide.

"Calvin, Albert says you were in charge of the pass—"

"Don't look at me," Calvin blurted.

As we spent precious minutes passing the buck, the G4 maintained its course to a landing strip in Khartoum in the heart of Sudan, where we'd be met by armed rebels, where we would be landing in the middle of the night, and where, to say the least, *we would need our passports.*

Then I heard a voice from up front.

"I have *my* passport," the pilot muttered.

The next step was obvious: apologize profusely. Minutes ago I had demanded that the pilot take off. Now I was asking him to turn around. As we circled back for the passports, I didn't know his exact feelings at that moment, but it's fair to assume the pilot's spine was in the upright and locked position.

Prior to the flight, I released an optimistic statement.

"Paul Salopek . . . is a talented and respected journalist who was attempting to do his job telling the story of the people, culture, and history of the sub-Saharan region known as the Sahel." I wanted it known, in no uncertain terms: "Paul Salopek is clearly not a spy."

I had to admit, however, that it wasn't so clear. His ironclad innocence may have been evident to me, and to his wife, Linda, and to Ann Marie Lipinski, his editor at the *Chicago Tribune*— both of whom I had asked to join the trip—but it wasn't so obvious to his captors, for a few good reasons. For starters, when he was detained, Salopek was carrying two United States passports and satellite maps of the conflict area in Darfur. While carrying two passports is fairly common practice among journalists—during apartheid, for example, it would often help not to have a South Africa stamp when heading into black-controlled African countries—it does arouse a kind of cloak-and-dagger suspicion. And of the Darfur maps, it's fair to say the Sudanese who were holding Salopek did not consider that he might have been using the maps to *avoid* trouble, not to start some.

Another obstacle involved Salopek's traveling companions. He had been detained along with his interpreter, Suleiman Abakar Moussa, and his driver, Idriss Abdulraham Anu, both citizens of Chad, the neighboring country to the west of

Sudan, at their point of entry. And on what was already a dangerous trip, the latter two men came with their own dangerous baggage.

First off, although interpreter Suleiman Abakar Moussa was a veteran translator for a number of high-profile journalists who traveled to Sudan, he didn't actually exist. Moussa's real name was Daoud Hari, and he was not the helpful native of Chad he claimed to be. Rather, he was a Sudanese citizen who operated under the assumed name so he could work in Chad, where only Chadian workers can be employed. By the time Salopek hired him, Hari had already made six trips into Sudan, often for journalists who had been critical of the Sudanese government. His reputation had been sealed: If not a spy, he was at least an agitator. That was the first strike for Salopek; while he hadn't in fact been writing "false news," he had been traveling with a translator who was using a false name.

Strike two was their driver, Idriss Abdulraham Anu, who chose as their method of transport a brand-new Toyota pickup truck. In the currency of drug runners and rebel fighters, a pickup is more valuable than a Bentley. In Hari's own memoir years later, he wrote about his suspicion that the truck had as much to do with their detainment as anything else—and what's more, that the charges of espionage, and the threats of execution, were levied so the captors would appear to be protecting the country, not merely stealing a car. In any case, if Salopek had wanted to travel safely and undetected, he would have had better luck paddling through the desert in his trusty canoe.

As we began our descent into South Sudan—passports in hand—I well knew that I might have some more convincing to do. This might not be as quick a transaction as I wished.

I decided to pull out all the stops. I turned to Linda and told her, "When I go to see al-Bashir, it'll be only me in the room."

"Good," she said, almost trembling. "Because I don't think I can—"

"Unless"—I interrupted her—"unless I tell you to come in."

"What can I do?" she asked.

"Listen, you're nervous. I understand. But I've done a lot of these things." This seemed to put her slightly at ease. "This one isn't just about how many perks I can throw in. So I may want you to come in and make an appeal for the release of your husband. You need to let al-Bashir know how much you love him."

"Okay, I can do that."

"Great." I swallowed hard, and got to what I was aiming at. "And if you happen to start crying, it's okay. A little emotion might help."

"You want me to cry?" she asked.

"Well, it's either you or me, and if I start crying, that just means we're screwed."

"But I'm not a very emotional person."

"Can you try to become one by the time we see al-Bashir?" She said she'd try.

Then Ann Marie, ever the editor, spoke up. "Governor, if it helps get him out I can promise you I'll cry."

"I don't need you to cry."

"But I'd like to be in the room. I'd like to have something to write about."

I promised her I'd do my best to get her in to see al-Bashir. But as we landed in Africa, I reminded myself that we had to get back out in a hurry.

"Listen, we're not gonna stop at the casbah. We're not gonna stop at the souk. Ann Marie, if you take a picture, it better be a blurry one. We're on the move. We're gonna get in, get on with it, and get out. Before they change their minds."

When our wheels hit the tarmac, it was night. The large African sun had set on Khartoum hours before. But a friendly face was there to greet us: the American ambassador, Cameron Hume, who had visited Salopek with Congressman Shays. Hume had worked with me at the UN; he's not your typical diplomat and that's why we work so well together. And he came with news: Despite the late hour, President al-Bashir wanted to see us right away. The group was tired, but I was thrilled. I knew we had to strike right while the iron was hot.

We didn't bother to check in to the hotel in Khartoum. In fact, as our caravan made its way to the presidential palace, I told Ambassador Hume, "We may not need those hotel reservations after all." He was skeptical. He hadn't been privy to the assurances I had received from Ambassador Haroun. But as we arrived to meet President Omar al-Bashir, I could only hope that my intelligence was better than his.

At first, I met with the president one-on-one. I left my entourage, including Paul's wife, Linda, in another room. Of course, even though I was alone with the president, I didn't begin by saying, "Omar, I know this deal is precooked, so let's get on with it." It's never a good idea to be so presumptuous. Instead I said, "Mr. President, I appreciate our ten-year relationship," subtly reminding him that I gave his government credit for helping release the Red Cross workers a decade prior.

Even so, he then began to vent about US policy toward

Sudan, much as Kerubino had back in his chieftain's hut. "I try to be fair. The administration asks me to do something, I do it! But still, you put sanctions on me. I feel I have enemies in the US government, no matter how friendly I am."

Friendly is too strong a word, but I didn't point that out. Instead, I pled impotence.

"What can I do? I'm not in the administration," I told him.

"Ah, but I hear you might run." Mischief had crept into his tone.

"Listen," I said, "I'd like you to give me Salopek. And if you do, you'll be thanked, and I'll make the bad press you're getting disappear."

"Impossible," he insisted. "The press hates me."

I kept bringing up other reasons he should comply, and the president kept batting them down. I was beginning to think that the ambassador's implied promises were empty ones. Perhaps he had no clout after all.

I had no choice. I pulled an ace from my sleeve.

"Mr. President, I want you to meet Paul's wife."

Linda entered and told her touching story to the man in charge of the country detaining her beloved husband. And yes, she cried—although if I'm being honest, not as much as I'd hoped. I wasn't certain if it was effective, but I wanted to keep the pressure on. After asking Linda to leave, I leveled with al-Bashir. "Look, I don't have anything to give you except good press. And you'd be doing the right thing. Let's be honest: You've gotten everything you can out of this, and now you're starting to get a backlash. Do you need this aggravation?"

He laughed a little. I might be getting somewhere.

"Heck, maybe that's *why* the US treats you like an enemy, as you say. You're holding our journalist!"

He laughed again.

Feeling perhaps a little too confident, I gambled. "Plus, it's not like he's written bad stories about you."

"Oh, yes he did!" al-Bashir quickly retorted.

Oh shit. (Now I know why they tell prosecuting attorneys never to ask a question they don't already know the answer to. Turns out Salopek had been very critical of al-Bashir and the Sudanese government. For a veteran negotiator, I had committed an amateur mistake.)

Still, despite the misstep I was intent on satisfying one of my heartfelt rules: *Get the victory and go.*

"Look, are you going to give him to me or not? I really don't want to leave without him." I even appealed to our mutual vanity as public figures. "Plus, what will I tell people if I fail? You know how that looks!" The truth is, not many people even knew I was in Sudan. I could have slinked out, no worse for the wear.

Yet that tactic seemed to work.

After a moment, al-Bashir relented. "Okay," he said. "I'm going to release him to you." That's all I needed to hear. But al-Bashir continued. "I'm going to release him to you, but not for any of the reasons you mentioned."

Sure. Fine. No problem.

"I'm going to release him to you, but only because you're my friend. I get no benefit from this."

I disagreed, but wasn't about to belabor the point.

Remember: *Get the victory and go.*

"That's wonderful," I said. "Where is he?"

It was then that al-Bashir delivered the bad news that always seems to follow the good.

"No problem. He's only a thousand miles away."

My heart sank. I knew that a lot could happen in a thousand miles.

"How soon can you get him here?" I asked.

Get the victory and go.

"Oh no," al-Bashir laughed. "You have to go pick him up!" Although he was offering what I had asked for, he seemed to delight in the fact that he wasn't going to make it easy on me. One last hurdle, just to see me sweat.

"This way," he added, "you can see the problems in my country. You're a problem solver. Maybe you can solve some of my problems, too!"

I wasn't thrilled with al-Bashir's little game, and I had no idea how I was going to get to Salopek, but I knew better than to belabor the point. I gave al-Bashir a hearty handshake and a heartfelt thank-you. "Can I tell the press?" I asked.

"Not tonight. But tomorrow," he said.

Clearly, al-Bashir wasn't in the same hurry that I was. In fact, as I was leaving, he threw another obstacle in my path: "Wait!" he said. "You can have Salopek. But the other two stay."

Unacceptable.

"No, no, no," I told him.

"Yes, yes, yes," he insisted, claiming that their sentences of sedition demanded a larger—and lengthier—punishment.

"But Omar," I leveled with him. "I'm a politician. I can't take the white guy, and then leave the two black guys behind! How would that look?" I asked.

I knew it was a desperate move—pleading race politics, rather than rational reason—but clearly al-Bashir was amused. After a moment, he started laughing uproariously. "Okay, okay, okay," he said. He waved his arm above his head as a way of wrapping up the matter: "You can have them. But go! Get them out of here!"

Finally, I thought. *A fellow politician who understands the need to get a move on.*

Still, it was on me to make it happen. After I left the room,

I asked Ambassador Hume how we could fly across Africa—right now, today. His first response was understandable—"This isn't exactly in our budget"—but I knew he understood the gravity of the situation.

"Look, we're rescuing a hostage here," I said. I impressed upon him the Richardson rule—*Get the victory and go.* The sooner the better. And I didn't have to say that it was the right thing to do.

Ambassador Hume understood. "I'll get it done," he said.

Thankfully, he arranged for a charter flight into the interior of Sudan for the next morning. That was all I needed to hear, but my aide Calvin, who has an outsize fear of flying, had another request: "The governor requires safe planes. For his safety."

"For *my* safety?" I joked. "For *your* safety!"

Calvin laughed.

As did al-Bashir, who heard the exchange.

The next morning, we met up with a junior officer in the US consul who knew precisely (or as precisely as one could) where Salopek was being held, and together we boarded a small twenty-seater plane to Darfur.

As much as I wanted nothing more than to make it a quick visit, I was advised that the first order of business on our arrival should be to meet the governor of the area, so that there would be no misunderstandings when we went to retrieve Salopek. We frantically arranged an appointment and hurried to his office. *Get the victory and go.*

The only problem: When we arrived, the governor was nowhere to be found. Even though we had made it clear we were coming, and had been granted permission to arrive, his staff insisted he hadn't been expecting us. The office was chaotic. People streamed in and out. Unfortunately, none of them were the governor.

"Do you know when the governor is coming back?" I asked.

"Not only do we not know when he's coming back," one staffer said with too much of a grin, "we don't know where he is!"

I told our consul we couldn't afford to wait and insisted that we head to the prison even without the governor's blessing. It knew it was a risk, but I also knew that waiting too long is even riskier. Our embassy vehicles looked official enough; hopefully they, and the few Sudanese locals we'd hired for security, would carry a little weight with the prison guards.

The guards were very polite, but uncooperative. The head of the prison greeted us but insisted he had heard nothing of an American governor being given permission to show up at his prison and make off with his celebrity prisoner. I implored him to call the president and hear it for himself.

"No," he said.

"No?"

"No, the president should call me!"

Oh great. I was not only in the middle of Sudan, I was in the middle of a power struggle.

"Am I at least in the right prison?" I asked.

"How would I know?" he said.

Naturally. "Well, tell me. Are Paul Salopek and the others here?"

"Oh yes, they're right over there!" he said, pointing at a cell not too far away.

So close, and yet so far.

After an hour of getting nowhere, a local political leader— another "chief" with no authority whatsoever—showed up and repeated the refrain: He'd received no word about our visit. Another hour passed. I was getting despondent.

Then came the you-gotta-be-kidding-me last straw: The

warden started showing me a collection of rugs and jewelry, hoping perhaps that I was in the mood to buy.

Enough!

I demanded that he call the president. "You have to have his number." I tried to play on his ego. "Certainly a powerful man like you has his number."

He disappeared into another room. After a few minutes he returned and gave me news I wanted to hear. "The president says yes."

Great. We've gotten our victory. Now we go!

I stood up and started to make my way to the cell, only to be told by the head of prisons that even a presidential pardon isn't the last step: It has to be certified by the local judge.

I prayed that the judge was *very* local—as in, just down the block.

No luck. Not only was the judge not local, he was out of town, and no one seemed to know quite where. All they knew: "He won't be coming back until Monday."

I bluffed. I told him that I had to meet with the president again, so they shouldn't do anything to upset *his* tight schedule. All of a sudden, the warden was in a much more helpful mood. He dispatched his assistant with a simple instruction: *Find the judge.*

Two hours later, there was still no sign of His Honor. As I sat in the prison, mere feet away from Salopek, I was beginning to feel like I was serving a sentence myself. To make matters worse, the head of prisons chose to bide the time by delivering some bad news: As written, the presidential pardon was only for Salopek, not for his interpreter or driver. I was tempted to use the same argument I had with President al-Bashir, but I didn't think it would have the same pull. Instead I just said, "The deal is for three." I was out of arguments.

Thankfully, the head of prisons revealed that the judge—still nowhere to be found—had the authority to increase the pardon to address all three men. "Great," I said. "Let's go find the judge."

"No," the local politician said. "I'll go do it."

And with that, he took off—in the opposite direction of the previous man. I wasn't exactly optimistic. So we spent the next few hours twiddling our thumbs, being sold rugs, and evading the occasional wild animal that would ramble through the prison lobby. Paul's wife, Linda, was beginning to lose faith, and I couldn't blame her. I too thought perhaps our luck was running out. *Are they even going to find the judge, let alone convince him to second-guess the president?*

Then after another hour: Out walked Salopek. They had set him free.

Whatever phone call it was that needed to be placed had been placed, yet only for Salopek.

Paul and his wife embraced and went into the corner to spend some overdue time together. After a while, I inquired about the other two men. Paul told us they had been separated, and that one of them was being badly mistreated. In fact, both Hari and Anu were being badly treated—they were malnourished and repeatedly beaten. Salopek too had been starved, although he had avoided the worst physical punishment.

I explained that the pardon appeared to apply only to him. The others were still behind bars. Without missing a beat, he said, "I won't leave without them."

"I understand," I replied. "But if push comes to shove, is that your position?"

"Yes," he said.

I had never contemplated the alternative, but it was good to know his position. I wanted to get the victory and go, but leaving without the other two men would have meant it wasn't a victory at all.

Just then, we heard the slamming of brakes outside. The local politician—I *still* don't know who he was or what position he held—had returned in his tiny two-car caravan. He jumped out of his car and raised his arms in victory. "I got it!" he yelled. "I've got it for three!"

Yes, I hugged him.

The guards went to fetch the other two men. And sure enough, they did not look good. They were thin, glassy-eyed, weak. But despite their condition, they were also grateful. Hari made his way past a goat and hugged me. "Thank you," he said. "You saved my life."

I didn't even take the time to accept the compliment. "Let's get out of here!" I insisted.

Linda, Paul's wife, pointed to the rugs and the jewelry and asked, "Shouldn't we buy some of this stuff as a gesture of goodwill?"

The only gesture I wanted to make was the move to the door. *Get the victory and go.*

"No!" I laughed. "The plane is waiting!"

And just then, as if we were characters in a French farce, in walked . . . THE GOVERNOR. Mr. Nowhere to Be Found was suddenly shaking my hand.

He not only insisted on greeting everyone and getting an update on what had transpired all day, but also made a very unwelcome suggestion: a dinner to honor the occasion.

Clearly, he didn't understand that all we wanted was to flee as quickly as possible. I was convinced we were never going to leave that country.

I turned to Ambassador Hume, who already knew what I was thinking. "He'd be insulted if we didn't accept," he whispered.

I turned back to the governor and said, "One hour!"

We went to his residence, and I did my best to make conversation with the governor. I put on my diplomatic hat and we talked politics. As the hour wrapped up, he gave me a blanket, and as everyone watched me accept it, I didn't mind too much if I appeared rude. I insisted that I had to get back to my legislature.

"Because they're a pain in the ass, right?" he asked.

"Yes, because they're a pain in the ass."

This, he seemed to understand.

Finally, after what had seemed like the longest day of my life, our caravan zoomed back to the remote landing strip and we boarded the plane.

You might think that was the end of the story. That it was indeed a happy ending. You'd be only partly right.

As we leveled off, one of the Africans, who clearly wasn't used to eating a full meal, vomited in my lap.

Aw, what the hell. A small price for victory, I say.

This past January, Paul Salopek started a seven-year trek around the world to imitate the migration of early humans out of Africa. He plans to walk more than twenty thousand miles. Given how long things take in Africa, I might suggest that he run.

Fidel Castro:
OUR CUBAN MISSION CRISIS

ON AN EARLY TRIP TO CUBA, during my last term as a congressman from New Mexico, Cuban strongman Fidel Castro and I came to an agreement that helps thousands of Cubans and remains one of the proudest accomplishments of my negotiating career: the Richardson Agreement.

For many years, the Cuban government would charge any Cuban who emigrated to the United States an exorbitant amount of money to do it, effectively making the proposition—a shot at the American Dream—financially impossible. At the time of my arrival, the penalty was a prohibitive $600, a fee the average Cuban living in poverty simply couldn't afford. By the time of my departure, Castro had agreed to halve that fee to $300 for up to a thousand hopeful Cuban émigrés each year—still expensive, but it made the American Dream an American possibility for many more Cubans. To this day, it is still known as the Richardson Agreement—and I am as happy to have my name plastered on that pact as I am on any plaque or honorary degree.

Which is why I'm willing to say, or rather, to admit: Fidel

Castro and I have a lot in common. Of course I realize that American politicians don't win many elections if they go around saying, "You know something? Fidel Castro and I have a lot in common." But the fact remains: Fidel Castro and I have a lot in common.

Cozying up to the dictator who has long held command of one of the most enduring and confrontational communist countries on the planet—a man who infamously antagonized the United States by hosting a battery of Russian nuclear missiles just ninety miles from American shores—isn't exactly a good electoral platform. Castro has, after all, frustrated the world a few times over. For starters, he played a bit of a bait-and-switch game right from his very entrance onto the world stage. Although he arrived in Havana on the back of a tank, he initially proclaimed himself something of a reasonable democrat, open to the challenges and the charms of the United States. It wasn't long before a different truth emerged: He was yet another pro-Soviet communist, a willing puppet of Moscow. And he lived a stone's throw from Miami. (That is, if you can throw a stone ninety miles, a feat Fidel would probably argue some of his prized baseball stars could pull off with ease. A few, he'd insist, might even be able to bean someone in Sarasota.)

Then, over thirteen anxious days in 1962, he brought the world closer to nuclear war than anyone ever has when he allowed Soviet premier Nikita Khrushchev to build missile bases capable of lobbing sixty nuclear warheads onto the American mainland.

So yes, Fidel Castro has been a frustrating, dangerous man, to say the least.

And yet, he and I have almost always gotten along. Despite his communist proclivities and his dictatorial style—to be sure, I am no fan of his politics nor of the cruel iron fist he wielded to keep his population repressed and despairing—I've generally felt ours was a good working relationship.

It helps that he and I are similar in many ways. I've never shrunk from the obvious parallels between myself and the man with the outsize personality who ruled the island country for more than a half century.

It further helps, of course, that most of our common traits are superficial, and therefore politically harmless. We're both large men with large appetites. We both love a good cigar. We both have the capacity to give longer speeches than some members of our respective audiences might wish. Castro is famous for wearing his olive-green military dress as if it were his pajamas, anywhere and everywhere, like a sign to everyone that he means business. For my part, there is a beloved blue blazer—my own *negotiation uniform*, if you will—that still hangs in my closet. (After two decades of world travels, it's threadbare, but I don't dare part with it.) If I'm being totally honest, both of us sometimes overlook the finer details of our own, let's say, *personal presentation*. Which is to say, I've been known not to notice a coffee stain on my tie for most of a day, whereas Fidel—well, I'll just say it—has more dandruff than anyone I've ever met. His shoulders are practically snow peaks. I'd like to chalk it up to us having more important things on our minds.

Perhaps the most significant bond—one that is the stuff of cinematic tearjerkers, one that brings even estranged fathers back together with estranged sons—is that we both love baseball. In fact, we're both not only huge fans of baseball, but also avid players. And pretty good ones, in our respective days. On one trip to Cuba, I even took in a local game so I could tell Fidel what I thought of his talent. Later, I reported my findings. "They were all offense. Terrible defense." He laughed, but he wasn't about to admit any flaws in the Cuban style of play. "You must have gone to the wrong game," he chortled.

Thanks to this personal touch, we've had a very good working relationship. In any negotiation, it never hurts to emphasize the similarities between you and your counterpart, even if you fail to agree on even the most fundamental substance of what you're negotiating. The more you have in common, and the more you reinforce and draw attention to those commonalities rather than let them go unspoken, the more common ground you'll likely be able to reach. Thus it has been with Castro and me; together, over the years, we have had the will to work together, and we both feel we have achieved very real results benefiting both our countries.

Perhaps our greatest success was in 1996, a month after my visit to strike the Richardson Agreement, when I traveled back to Cuba as a member of the House Intelligence Committee. It wasn't a social visit. Dozens of dissidents had been rounded up and thrown in a Havana prison. Castro's prisons have had a reputation for decades, never good. Prior to the trip, I had been assured by the Cuban ambassador to the UN, Fernando Remírez de Estenoz, that if I arrived in person—and asked nicely—Castro might let me return with "four or five" jailed dissidents in tow. I had provided Remírez with a list of ten that I hoped to free. It was an opening bid in what I knew would be pure negotiation. Half that number would be considered a victory.

A decade earlier, in 1984, Jesse Jackson had had great success on this front as part of what he called a "moral offensive" he had launched around the world, negotiating directly with Castro and returning home with a whopping forty-nine dissidents he had convinced Castro to release from Cuban jails. For my part, when *mi amigo* Fidel offered me a mere three after a two-hour meeting with him in Havana, I couldn't help but appeal to my Hispanic brother.

"But Fidel, you gave Jesse forty-nine! And you're only offering me three? You gave the black guy almost fifty, but you're giving the Hispanic guy *three*? *¿Solamente tres?* You're gonna make me look bad."

Yes, it may seem a cheap negotiation trick—appealing to our mutual ethnicity—but if it had worked, it would have been a rich reward. I was happy to try anything.

Fidel laughed at my ploy, but didn't budge. Three it would remain.

I was grateful, as were Carmen Arias Iglesias, an activist who had spoken out in favor of the US embargo restricting travel to and trade with Cuba; Luis Grave de Peralta, who had supported Arias in her position; and Eduardo Ramón Prida Gorgoy, a physicist who had vocally supported the adoption of a free market in Cuba. They were free.

Unfortunately, the families of the three freed dissidents were still stuck in Cuba. I urged Castro to release them soon after our departure, and he seemed to consider the possibility. So, naturally, I advised Grave, Prida, and Arias to say nothing that might offend Castro when we landed in Miami and held a press conference. There was still negotiation work to be done. Prida and Arias complied, but to my dismay Grave couldn't restrain himself, and he spent much of the press conference telling reporters what he really thought of Castro. Not surprisingly, while some of Arias's and Prida's relatives left Cuba soon after, Grave's relatives had no such luck.

There's an obvious lesson here that applies even in negotiations with far lower stakes. *Don't insult your counterpart— even unintentionally—as you walk out the door.* Even if you're the victor, even if you have achieved your goal, never forget that there will be another goal tomorrow. There's always another negotiation, so while a quick, tossed-off insult may feel good in the moment, it won't feel good in the morning.

That's one reason why I have never insulted Fidel the man, even while I have disagreed with Castro the strongman. The favor has been returned: He's always treated me with dignity and respect, even when he has rebuffed my efforts to negotiate. And although he is, infamously, one of the reasons the world came far too close to global thermonuclear annihilation, and a man with terrible dandruff to boot, he's also—well, I'll just say it—something of a friend.

I recognize the absurdity. I also recognize that some Cuban Americans would not want to hear an American politician saying something positive about Castro. But as I've said— and this is a huge lesson that bears repeating—working relationships, even with a rival or enemy, must be maintained and fed. That's how things get done. No relationship? No dialogue? *No results.* Period. There's no denying that Castro and I have had a reliable and effective working relationship over the past few decades. And somehow, miraculously, I still managed to win a few elections over the years. (Perhaps I'm just that good of a politician.)

Of course, the relationship between our two countries hasn't been quite as congenial. Since 1982, the US Department of State has designated the tiny island as one of the few "state sponsors of terrorism"—a list of troublemaking nations on which even recalcitrant North Korea, a member of the so-called axis of evil, is no longer featured. Only Iran, Sudan, and Syria share Cuba's official black mark, which imposes strict, and intentionally crippling, trade sanctions and other punishments. Despite Castro's insistence that Cuba no longer supports armed rebellion and insurgencies abroad, the State Department contends otherwise. Namely, that his government hasn't severed its ties with either the rebels of the Revolutionary Armed Forces of Colombia (FARC) or the Basque Euskadi Ta Askatasuna (ETA) separatists in Spain. Castro, they say, still has his finger in a lot of distasteful and dangerous pies.

As a result, there is no official operating relationship between the United States and Cuba. And there remains no American embassy in Havana, even though it could be argued that an embassy might have been helpful during those tense thirteen days in 1962. Instead, there is merely what's awkwardly known as the US Interests Section, a large, intimidating building (that, it must be said, looks suspiciously like an embassy, and acts like an embassy, and is certainly guarded like an embassy) just across the main oceanfront drive—the Malecón—from the Atlantic Ocean. It's a prime piece of beachfront real estate, so close to the water that on windy days when the surf is up, the waves often crash all the way over the road—just as they did in the days of Graham Greene's *Our Man in Havana*—and lap at the US Interests Section's front door.

It is also ground zero for the propaganda wars between democracy and communism. As it happens, the US Interests Section butts up against a large ocean-side plaza where Cuban politicians often stage rallies to trumpet the glories of their Cuban-style communism. Seizing an opportunity to trumpet the glories of democracy to those same protesters and politicians, the Americans installed a large electronic ticker in the plaza-facing fifth-floor windows of the Interests Section building to display a continuous stream of messages directly to the Cuban people. Nothing too jingoistic, but considering the venue, hard to miss. Among the reported messages: *The United States wishes the Cuban people a Happy New Year.* Harmless perhaps, but the Cubans nonetheless saw this as a devious and underhanded tactic and engaged in an amusing game of one-upmanship themselves. Between the building and the plaza they installed a vast array of 150 towering flagpoles that can be deployed like a curtain whenever necessary to obscure the view of the ticker entirely—essentially, a wall of flags. The message was clear: No Cuban enjoying a political rally in the plaza would ever again be forced to suffer the indignity of an American wishing them a happy New Year.

I can't deny that this fraught relationship between Cuba and the United States has occasionally, and perhaps inevitably, seeped into my relationship with Castro. After a visit of mine in 1996, I learned from Cuban friends that Fidel felt that I hadn't done enough to warn the US government about his concern over a group of Cuban exiles in Miami known as Brothers to the Rescue, who flew planes over Cuban air space. Castro felt they were taunting the Cuban government and acting provocatively. I had passed Castro's message on, but when Cuban gunships shot down one these planes, the US/Cuban relationship soured even further.

The most absurd example of Fidel and me "playing the game" occurred when we both attended the inauguration of Hugo Chávez in Venezuela—who, by the way, was another dictator who had an impressive amount of stamina in his day. His inaugural speech alone lasted four hours. We knew Chávez was a leftist, but at the time we still thought we could deal with him, so my attendance at the gala event was approved by the American State Department.

The reception was held in a fancy outdoor castle in Caracas. When our ambassador learned that both Castro and I would be in the same castle at the same time, he just about blew a gasket. His overreaction was comical. The instructions he gave me just kept getting nuttier, especially considering two facts: one, I knew Castro well, and two, the world already *knew* I knew Castro well. Still, he was adamant: *You cannot greet him,* he told me. *If he puts his hand out, you cannot shake it. If he smiles at you, don't smile back. If he tries to hug you, run. If he calls your name, pretend you don't speak Spanish.* Oh, I may be exaggerating, but not by much.

Luckily, Castro knew the bind I was in, and he respected it, so he didn't press the matter. What resulted was beyond silly. Even as one of my handlers, Rebecca Gaghen, tried to maneuver me away from him, the castle was only so big. And when we eventually bumped into each other in the crowded courtyard, he simply nodded at me in silence. I nodded back.

But we didn't dare shake hands.

Can you imagine the hell that would have broken loose had we shaken hands?!

Yeah, neither can I.

It's all the more ludicrous when you realize how often Castro and I have worked together, and how—usually—we have achieved real successes.

Although *success* doesn't describe my most recent trip to Cuba. No, my most recent trip to Cuba was, for lack of a more charitable description, a complete failure. In September 2011, I returned to Cuba after Fidel had handed off control of the country to his younger brother Raúl. I don't know Raúl as well as I know his more colorful older brother, but that didn't stop me, and I once again returned to Havana in the hope of securing the release of a high-profile detainee.

Alan Gross was an American contractor for the United States Agency for International Development (USAID). He had been deployed to Cuba, and then detained, after his attempts to install satellite Internet networks for the island's small Jewish community. Frustrated with what they saw as a subversion attempt, and furious that Gross was connecting Cubans to communications networks that the Cuban regime couldn't control, the Cubans accused Gross of a trio of sins: espionage, working for the US government, and trying to subvert the state. On December 3, 2009, the night before he was due to return home from Cuba to his wife in suburban Maryland, Gross opened his door to four hulking Cuban security agents.

He's been detained ever since, assigned a fifteen-year prison sentence. It's a sad story. Both his mother and his daughter have cancer. He's also reported to be quite sick. Recent pictures suggest that he's lost more than a hundred pounds while in detainment. Not surprisingly, after giving him what must have been a cursory medical evaluation, Cuban officials deny he has cancer and have accused the United States of lying to garner sympathy and make them look malicious. They say he's a spy who deserves his full sentence.

One hopes it's not a life sentence.

In fairness, the US State Department has been cagey about what exactly Gross was doing in Cuba. His mission, which had been approved during the George W. Bush administration, was part of a controversial—some have said unduly provocative—program designed by USAID and created by the 1996 passage of the Cuban Liberty and Democratic Solidarity (LIBERTAD) Act, otherwise known as Helms-Burton, after its sponsors then-senator Jesse Helms and then-representative Dan Burton. The Helms-Burton Act has long been a thorn in Cuba's side, since it specifically allots funding for creating various means for Cubans to access information without the Cuban government's permission, in the grand hope back then of fostering the fall of Fidel Castro. Or, in the language of the act, "a peaceful transition to representative democracy and a market economy."

It goes without saying that I'm all for the free flow of information and peaceful transitions to democracy, as any leader who's not paranoid or despotic should be. But as the powers that be in Cuba see it, working under the auspices of the Helms-Burton Act, in any shape or manner, is a crime.

Honestly, whatever work Gross had been up to—benign or malignant—was not my concern. My concern was to get him released. And on this matter, I made a number of mistakes.

I suppose my first mistake was trusting the word of the Cuban ambassador, Jorge Alberto Bolaños Suárez—a very nice older man who had been in the Cuban Foreign Ministry since the early '60s—but one who talked a bigger game than he played. It's a key factor in any pre-negotiation: Deal only with someone who has juice. *Don't take no from someone who can't say yes* is often said. Well, the corollary is also true: *Don't take yes from someone who only has the power to say no*. If they're not authorized to deal with you, don't deal with them.

Anyhow, Bolaños indicated I'd improve my chances to get Gross's release if I brought along some incentives. Unfortunately, it ultimately became clear that Bolaños no longer had the ear of Cuban power. He was more closely aligned with Fidel than with Raúl. Yet I trusted him—to my chagrin—and so I proposed a long list of diplomatic goodies that I knew the

Cubans would appreciate: most notably, earnest efforts to remove Cuba from the state sponsors of terrorism list, allowing certain Cuban spies imprisoned in Florida access to their families, cooperation on stemming environmental damage on the island, and helping the Cubans fund much-needed hospitals. No promises, no guarantees, but honest efforts.

In return, I asked for a meeting with new president Raúl Castro.

Bolaños could only guarantee a meeting with Bruno Rodríguez Parrilla, the foreign minister. Still, knowing that Rodríguez was involved in the negotiations over Gross, and that he and I had previously worked together, I felt confident enough to accept the arrangement.

So confident did I feel, in fact, that I made my second mistake. In high-level negotiations, at certain points it's often a good idea to use publicity to advance your cause—to announce to the world what you're up to and what you hope to achieve. This was not one of those points. Yet I alerted CNN's Wolf Blitzer that I was headed to Cuba and I might get lucky and bring Alan Gross back. He, in turn, told the world of my plans via CNN International. And in 2011, even though Cubans might have been cut off from much of the televised world, they could access CNN International. So after flying into Havana and stepping into the lobby of the Hotel Nacional—where most diplomats stay and where most reporters, often having nothing better to do, linger and swap stories and scoops at the bar—I was barraged with cameras and microphones. I had just arrived and hadn't even had my first meeting. It was too much publicity, too soon. I put myself in my opposing negotiators' shoes: *Boy, Richardson is cocky,* they must have thought. *Just who does he think he is?*

It's an easy lesson learned the hard way: Don't get out ahead of the negotiation, and don't make public assumptions about the willingness of your co-negotiator to play ball. Put another way, if you're hoping to ask a favor of your brother, don't tell your sister it's a done deal. I cornered the Cubans, and they weren't happy about it.

After checking in with the US Interests Section and consulting with the chief of mission—always a good idea to keep your base up to speed, lest you need their help in a pinch—I knew I needed to smooth things over with the Cubans quickly, so off I went to meet with Bruno.

Bruno Eduardo Rodríguez Parrilla was a man I had dealt with a number of times prior to our meeting in Cuba. Before becoming the Cuban foreign minister, he was the country's permanent representative to the United Nations when I was US ambassador there, and I was certainly glad to know him at that time. He would often slip me cigars, which I would smoke in the United Nations lounge to the envy of many of my UN colleagues (and to the scorn of some). As I arrived at the guest house where we were to meet, I wondered whether our relationship would continue to be fruitful.

He greeted me with a big smile and a bigger hug. Setting the tone right away, he was wearing a comfortable guayabera and scoffed at my stuffy suit, which he said was unbecoming of a fellow Hispanic. On the one hand, I was relieved by his teasing. He clearly wanted this to be a cordial meeting, as did I. On the other, I could sense that the game of friendly one-upmanship— in other words, the negotiation—was already under way.

It was then that he offered me the usual pleasantry: a cigar. Of course, I accepted.

These kinds of small talk and gracious welcoming gestures are fundamental parts of negotiation at every level. It's vital to set the stage with a base of rapport—*how's your kids, how's your wife, how's your husband, how's your golf game*—before getting to the substance—*how's about we stop fooling around and you do what I ask.* Usually the smart move is to wait for your fellow negotiator to bring it up and move on to the heart of the matter. However, small talk can also wear thin, especially when you get a sense halfway through a meal that your hosts are merely stalling.

I chose the shortest cigar he had.

As the waiter poured us some wine, Bruno opened up. "Rich-ard-son!" he said.

I had noticed long ago that the Hispanic negotiators would call me by my last name—and overpronounce it—as a declaration of warmth.

"Rich-ard-son! *Dime lo que quieres decirme.*"

Tell me what you want to tell me.

It was the opening I had hoped for since finishing my small cigar, so I began to tell him what I had in mind: the release of the American contractor Alan Gross. But he interrupted me.

"Rich-ard-son! Let us talk about the politics in your country."

Even though it seemed an attempt to stall, it was a subject in which I was quite interested, so I let him continue.

"Tell me," he said. "Is Obama going to win reelection?" But before I could offer my perspective, he launched into his theories about Obama's chances. That's when I knew he was stalling: He just wanted to hear himself talk.

Now it was my turn to interrupt: "How's Raúl?" I asked.

He gave a cursory answer, then came back over the top.

"You think Obama is going to beat Romney?"

I realized the only way I was going to make progress was if I somehow used my answer to bring us to the matter at hand. "Yes, I think Obama's going to be reelected," I told him, "and you have to admit he's been good for Cuba–US relations. But," I said, "you guys aren't reciprocating."

He saw what I was aiming at, but he didn't bite.

The waiters served the soup.

We finished the soup.

The waiters served the fish.

We finished the fish.

They served the steak, and the wine, and the dessert.

All very delicious, but still nothing.

I had burned through the short cigar long ago; now my patience was growing even shorter.

Finally, even though he was my host—and even though it violates my principle that it's usually a good idea to let your fellow negotiator put things in motion—I abruptly brought up the subject of the American detainee.

"Let's talk about Gross," I said.

He again seemed reluctant to move on to such a weighty subject, but he let me lead the way.

"Okay," he said.

I outlined the various incentives I was empowered to offer. He was interested, but suspicious.

"Is this coming from the president?

No, I told him.

"Is this coming from the White House?"

No, I told him.

"Is this guaranteed by the State Department?!"

No, I told him.

I started to wonder if he was going to make his way all the way down the list of government agencies to the Office of Weights and Measures.

"Are you making all this up?" he asked.

I assured him I wasn't.

On the matter of removing Cuba from the terrorism watch list, he asked, "Can you sign a letter assuring that?"

I told him no, but that if he began the first step—releasing Gross—there's a very discrete process to apply to be removed.

"But it's not an actual commitment?" he asked, aghast.

I was beginning to see his side of the issue. Although I had come with incentives, I hadn't come with guarantees. It must have sounded hollow.

I made a different appeal.

"Look, I worked my ass off to get you these. Work with me."

He wasn't exactly moved.

"Where did you get the idea that we are ready to give up Gross?" he asked. "All we know is you told Wolf Blitzer you were going to bring Gross home with you."

Ouch. He had a point. I had gotten too far out in front of the story, and had made promises in public I hadn't yet delivered in private.

"Your ambassador said this would happen!" I insisted. It wasn't a compelling argument, since I realized right there and then that invoking Bolaños's promise wasn't going to help.

I took yet another tack.

"Have you had a change in policy? Do you want to improve relations with us or not?" I asked.

"Oh, Rich-ard-son!" he replied. "We've been waiting sixty years to improve relations with you. And nothing's ever happened!"

"Bruno, this is not good. I'm going to go back to the Nacional and they're going to ask what we discussed. What do I tell 'em?"

"You tell them I said, 'What do you think we are? A third-world country?'"

I wanted to say that there are certain elements of Cuba that are somewhat third world: jailing political dissidents, for starters. But that would have been impolite.

"Are you going to give me Gross?" I asked, perhaps too directly.

He was just as direct: "No."

Not what I wanted to hear.

It was a definitive answer, but that didn't mean our negotiation was over. And there's a lesson there too: In a negotiation, even if you don't get the primary result you are asking for, there should always be some secondary negotiation points, so at the very least you can feel like the relationship has progressed and will stay fruitful.

"Okay then," I told him. "I have two other requests."

All he said in response: "I'll convey them."

"I want a meeting with Raúl. And I want to see Gross."

"I don't think this is possible," he said.

"Why not?"

"Because you didn't ask for it before."

"I'm asking for it now!" I laughed.

"*No es posible.* There are too many preparations that would need to be completed."

"Preparations? What preparations? We just jump in one of your fabulous old Plymouths and you take me to see him!"

"No, he's gotta be prepared to meet you, the facility has to be notified, it's too complicated to do in a hurry."

Weak arguments, all.

"Plus, I need to be in Venezuela in three hours!" he said.

He was clearly just throwing obstacles in my way.

"Why? So you can be with Chávez and the lefties?" I joked.

"Well, *yes,*" he said.

I was out of arguments.

"Bruno."

"Rich-ard-son!"

"Bruno!"

"Rich-ard-son . . . "

"Bruno, you know that I am going to have to go back and talk to the press, and they're going to know this didn't go well."

"You do what you have to do." He said nothing more.

I didn't go back to the Nacional, very aware that I was going to meet a gaggle of press, thanks to my earlier mistake. And I didn't know yet how I was going to spin this defeat. Instead my team and I went to a friend's house overlooking the Malecón. I was frustrated and feeling defeated.

You'll forgive the bad pun, but I was having a Cuban mission crisis.

I had been told that Josefina Vidal, a top Cuban diplomat in charge of US affairs, would be calling me with an official answer about my requests. I was trying to get my hopes back up; they had, after all, let human-rights groups and some members of the black congressional caucus visit.

When Josefina called, I didn't expect what she said.

"Aquí está Bruno."

Bruno is here.

And the news he delivered was bad: "One, the president can't see you—he is too busy."

That's okay. At this point I was more interested in seeing Gross.

"And two," he said, "you can't see Gross."

Bruno!

"Okay, Bruno, you leave me no choice. I'm going to have to go to the press with this." My team and I thought it was important not to let them get away with a complete stonewall. At this point, we were thinking that a little public pressure was our best—and maybe last—chance to soften them.

We called a press conference at the hotel. Not that we needed to—they were already there, drinking at the bar and waiting for some news to report. It was, by Cuban standards, a massive contingent—five cameras, ten print reporters, and what seemed like fifteen languages.

And I was upset. It's never a good idea to go before the cameras when your blood is boiling. So I made yet another mistake. I said in Spanish, "I came to try to negotiate for the release of Alan Gross, but they were not willing to negotiate. And so I call on the Cuban government to free Alan Gross, who I fear has become a political hostage."

I should have said *detainee*, not *hostage*. I went to bed cringing that I might have made a bad situation worse simply with one word.

Nonetheless, the next morning I received a call from Josefina. She delivered the news that I'd been summoned to speak with Dagoberto Rodríguez Barrera, a diplomat and the former chief of the Cuban Interests Section. I told my team, "Maybe there's a break in the case. Maybe they buckled."

So we hurried to another plush safe house for the meeting. I like Dagoberto, in part because his name is fun to say, and Dagoberto is the only Cuban who calls me "Beeeel." He usually greets me warmly. But on this morning, he was all business. The usual pleasantries were dispensed with and they asked me to sit down. It's pretty common wisdom that nothing good ever comes after you've been asked to sit down. It's never "Sit down, you won the lottery."

But I didn't know just what kind of bad news I was in for. And that's when Dagoberto began to read off a piece of paper. *"Tenemos una comunicación oficial."* We have an official statement.

"We would like you to leave the country."

Yikes. I knew I might have offended them with my *hostage* slipup, but I have to say I didn't see this coming.

He continued reading: "We have talked about Alan Gross and, as you know, the discussions have not been productive. And we would like you to leave Cuba because the negotiations have not worked."

And with that, he just smiled at me.

Needless to say, no one wants to be ejected from a country, even with a smile. It stings. So I said, "No."

Not sure they expected that.

"I want you to know," I continued, "that I'm not going to leave until I see Alan Gross in the hospital. I'm not leaving Cuba voluntarily. If you want to eject me, go ahead."

It was a bold statement, and I knew I couldn't quite back it up. Was I really willing to stay in Cuba forever? No reason both Gross and I had to be detained, after all, even in a magnificent hotel like the Nacional. Heck, I knew I couldn't afford it!

Still, I went back to the hotel and told the press what I had declared to Dagoberto. I told my team we might be there for a while, so they should call the airlines and cancel our flights home, and I was careful to tell them as well that they shouldn't make other flight reservations, because surely the Cubans were monitoring our phones and would know if we just pushed them back a day or two.

So we stayed. They didn't try to eject me. But neither did they let me see Gross. It was a game of stalemate, but to mix a metaphor, they held all the cards. After a few days, the Cubans communicated with the State Department, and the State Department told me they didn't think the Cubans were going to change their position.

No meeting with Gross.

No meeting with Raúl.

But they did come back with a new demand. "We'll take the Cuban Five." The Cuban Five is a group of intelligence agents who were sent to Miami in the 1990s to infiltrate Cuban exile groups. They were arrested and have been in jail for fifteen years. And yet they are not forgotten. Spend a few days in Havana and you'll see a hundred billboards and posters describing them as antiterrorist heroes and insisting on their safe return.

To exchange them for Gross seems on its face an unfair trade. The Cuban Five are clearly spies who had done some real damage—the spy leader, Gerardo Hernández, also provided intelligence to Havana that led to the 1996 crash of two civilian airplanes over the Florida Straits. And a case can definitely be made—and Washington seemed intent on making it—that Gross was merely an unwitting development worker who got in over his head trying to help Cuban Jews. Whether that's true is beside the point. A five-for-one trade doesn't add up.

Anyhow, I wasn't about to try to negotiate the release of spies right then and there. I had no choice but to return to America with my tail between my legs.

I'd insisted I wouldn't leave without Gross. Ultimately, I left without Gross.

Later I was told that the Cubans actually *were* planning to release Gross to me when I arrived if I brought along some goodies, but after a few high-level meetings in which Raúl was told, "You can't give this guy up easily," they concocted the Cuban Five scheme. Frankly, I don't know if I believe that. They seemed from the start not to want to play along.

Regardless, I had failed in my negotiation, a few times over.

I had made rookie mistakes. I had antagonized my negotiating partners by going to the press too early, I had used language that a diplomat should know better than to use, and in a fit of pique, I had stomped my feet and said *I'm not leaving until you give me what I want.*

But my failure can be your victory, because there are important lessons to be learned from my mistakes that can—and should—be applicable to even the most workaday negotiations.

So going forward, let's you and I agree that you should never be cocky about getting your negotiating partners to buckle under your will. It just makes them defensive.

Let's agree you should never be careless about the language you use to describe things they could be prickly about. It might offend them.

And let's agree you should never make a threat you know you can't deliver on. It might get you ejected from a country.

Let that be our new Richardson Agreement.

The Congo:

AND THE LORD SAID, "LET'S DO THIS!"

IN 2011, I WAS CALLED IN to stop a civil war.

That may be putting too fine a point on it—and is definitely giving me far too much credit—although that was how it was put to me. It's flattering that anyone might think I have the power to do something so momentous, although even the misplaced vote of confidence didn't take any of the pressure off. Still, as I landed in the heart of Africa, it's fair to say that nothing quickens the mind like stepping off a plane into what could soon turn out to be crossfire.

The Democratic Republic of the Congo, or DRC—often referred to as simply *the Congo,* usually in ominous tones in newscasts and print reports detailing the latest tally of mass killing—is one of the more treacherous places on Earth. Even its genesis was violent. The Congo as we know it now was birthed in 1997 as a product of armed insurrection, when the forces of Laurent-Désiré Kabila stormed Kinshasa and ousted

Mobutu Sésé Seko. In one of those hapless attempts to rebrand the country—*Nothing to see here, move along*—Kabila changed the name of his new home from Zaire back to the Democratic Republic of the Congo, which it hadn't been called since 1971.

As Shakespeare might have said, a rose by any other name still is the home to untold bloodshed.

I know that because I was there when it happened.

That year—1997—in my capacity as US ambassador to the United Nations, I had been sent by President Clinton and secretary of state Madeleine Albright to warn Mobutu in no uncertain terms that his days were numbered as the leader of Zaire. He had ruled for more than thirty years, and his government had weakened substantially. So had he, from prostate cancer. (Amusingly, the country's flashy new currency had been nicknamed "prostates" by the locals who suspected they were only printed to help defray Mobutu's medical bills.) So when I met with Mobutu, I was direct: "You can leave with dignity and your money, or you can leave as a carcass," I told him. "If you think this is going to turn out well for you, you're living in a dream world."

I also was charged with arranging a meeting between Mobutu and Kabila, in an attempt to make any handover of power as peaceful as possible. Both men were amenable to a meeting, but Kabila made a demand that one often only hears in comic books: We had to meet in international waters. (Never a dull moment in the diplomacy biz.)

The US State Department and Madeleine Albright thought it important that South African president Nelson Mandela and his deputy Thabo Mbeki be the peacemakers in this transition. That made sense; they had, after all, offered Mobutu exile in South Africa. Soon enough we landed in the port city of Pointe-Noire ("very *Heart of Darkness*," as an assistant described the place), and we were boarding the South African icebreaker ship *Outeniqua*. Our destination: the open ocean. Mobutu was with us; Kabila was not. He insisted on arriving later by helicopter.

As we waited for Kabila to arrive—and, frankly, as our fears that he'd never show up crept in—Mandela and I established a game plan. I suggested that I'd start things off and then hand the reins to the South African president. "I'll make the introductions, but you gotta get this done. You need to mediate this," I told him.

Mandela protested, "No, Congressman. I think you should mediate."

Mandela was clearly distracted; I couldn't get him to concentrate and couldn't understand why. Then one of his aides brought him a slip of paper. He retreated to a room next door and picked up a satellite phone call. I could hear his side of the conversation. It didn't take superpowers of deduction to realize he was talking to his fiancée, Graça Machel.

"I love you, darling." "I can't wait to see you, my sweetheart." "You are the love of my life."

What a negotiator.

When the call ended, Mandela returned to us a changed man. He grabbed Mobutu by the arm and said, "My dear friend, it is time to make peace."

Mobutu could feel the force in Mandela's voice; Mobutu agreed to hand over power immediately.

Like I said, what a negotiator.

Seriously, though, as much as I trust my own negotiating skills, I give deference to Nelson Mandela, a true master of the craft. He simply has a compelling air about him, a spirit. I myself have been charmed by it. Case in point: Earlier that summer, he and I had met in the Pointe-Noire airport for a brief meeting about these negotiations. But it wasn't all business; there was a traditional dance mounted for our entertainment. Mandela grabbed me by the arm too and said, "You must dance."

Understand, I'm not an attractive dancer. I tried to explain that to him. He shook his head no.

"You must dance. It is a symbolic gesture to the African people."

I danced. Badly. And that's the thing: When Nelson Mandela asks, you say yes.

Unfortunately, Kabila never showed up on the icebreaker (and yes, I was amused by our hosting negotiations on a ship designed to break ice). We made our way back to port, frustrated and annoyed. But we didn't give up; Thabo Mbeki and I separately flew to Angola to track him down. When Mbeki found him, he put the evasive rebel leader on the phone with Mandela.

I'm not sure what Mandela said. I suspect it was a far cry from "You are the love of my life." Rather, it was probably some version of "You must dance." Because Kabila danced. He met Mobutu soon after.

A few months later, Mobutu woke up from the "dream world" he had been living in and did leave his country, exiling himself to Morocco. Yet, I wasn't entirely certain that his replacement, Kabila, was going to be a better leader to end the civil strife in his war-torn country.

Turned out I was right. When I returned later that year, Kabila had already proved he was no benevolent leader, and that his Democratic Republic of the Congo was hardly democratic.

For starters, he almost kept us hostage, not offering us the fuel we knew we would need to return on our plane. He claimed there was none to be found. It would take some negotiating, but a form of subversive negotiation. I wasn't going to bargain directly with him. I would simply show him that this was a serious situation.

In moments like these, I make a scene. Often the only co-conspirators you can enlist are your own staffers and friends. In this case, I turned to special assistant Rebecca Gaghen and loudly announced, in front of everyone, that she'd be fired if she didn't find us the fuel we needed. The room was stunned.

"Yes sir," Rebecca replied, and scrambled out of the room.

Of course, she was in on it. I tend to "fire" my staffers quite often, although I rarely mean it. "Good morning, you're fired" . . . "Great work today, you're fired" . . . "Pick me up at 5 p.m., you're fired"—that kind of thing. It's just my way of showing affection. But that day I sounded deadly convincing in the meeting with Kabila. Not too long after, his staff miraculously found us some fuel.

Still, we now had to deal with a man who had become a true despot. On top of everything else, and far worse, were Kabila's provocative decisions to antagonize the international community. Namely, he was keeping at bay human-rights investigators who had been assigned by the United Nations to determine if Kabila's forces had committed genocide, killing tens of thousands of Hutu refugees from neighboring Rwanda. When I arrived, Kabila smelled an opportunity. He insisted that I help him get aid from the United States in return for allowing access to the inspectors. "Nice try," I told him. "Tell you what, you let investigators in first and then we'll talk." Surprisingly, he agreed to this—I had been fairly certain he was going to laugh me out of the room. But when the inspectors finally arrived, he still stonewalled them, not granting them access to anyplace outside of Kinshasa.

I returned for a third time that year and had almost the exact same experience. Kabila, in placating UN secretary general Kofi Annan, had in fact allowed inspectors back in, but once again their travel was restricted to the capital.

In the end, Kofi and I weren't the only ones frustrated by Kabila. Three years later, Kabila was murdered, ostensibly by one of his senior officers. The circumstances are murky, but one thing is clear: Apparently his officer was even more frustrated with Kabila's behavior than we were!

Kabila's murder didn't end the Kabila regime, however. His thirty-year-old son Joseph took the helm and drove the Congo even further into an economic and political morass.

It's a shame. It's a beautiful country. And it's been led for decades by selfish, dangerous, destructive leaders intent on turning it into a place few visitors would dare discover.

It was the son, Joseph, who caused the region more trouble in 2011—and thus me, too. It was because of his insecure position as president, and his increasingly desperate tactics to hold on to his power, that I was summoned to the Congo again. That year, there were a dozen or so presidential political parties with candidates running for office, and Joseph Kabila had refused to meet with any of them. The main opposition candidate, Étienne Tshisekedi, had already begun accusing Kabila of plans to rig the vote and was proposing that his supporters riot in the streets. It seemed a time to stay away from the region, frankly. But the nonprofit National Democratic Institute here in the States sensed that a civil war was brewing, so its president, Ken

Wollack, lit the bat signal, calling me to see if I could hop another flight to Kinshasa and try to corral Kabila into at least a meeting with his many opponents. Perhaps dialogue might reduce tensions.

I was a little skeptical, and more than a little reluctant; in truth, there were some who suspected I was a reason that Joseph was in power, and therefore I was somewhat tempted to keep my distance and stay out of it. And honestly, Ken's explanation for why I was the right man for the job didn't exactly reassure me. "All sides like you," he said. "Especially Kabila." Once again, I was in the absurd and unwelcome position of being told that a despot liked me. Although I was no longer in politics, I still balked at being a warlord's favorite diplomat. It doesn't exactly do wonders for my reputation.

Still I went. If I could help forestall a civil war, it was the least I could do.

When I arrived, the press covering my arrival was generally positive. Many remembered that I was the American ambassador who had helped get Mobutu out. (That he was replaced with a similarly ruthless despot seemed not to matter to them, to my relief.) And I immediately got to work, calling on all the major candidates to meet with me as soon as possible. I wanted to hear their complaints and what they had to say generally. It goes without saying that in any negotiation—with a warlord or a wife—the more reconnaissance you can get, the better off you'll be. You always want to be the best-informed person in the room, whether it be the conference room, the boardroom, or (let's be honest) the bedroom.

However, the Congo is also a big rumor mill, despite the

lack of modern communications technologies. There's not too much tweeting in the bush. So I'm not sure how the rumors spread—except perhaps that word of mouth (and only word of mouth) somehow travels very fast there. But this one particular rumor I had to squash if I was going to get anything done: Many believed that the real reason I was in the country was that the United States government wanted me to tell Kabila directly that he had to leave office—as I had done to Mobutu a decade earlier. Not true. So as I met with each candidate, I made sure they understood that I was there primarily to help stop the threat of increased violence, and to assist the electoral commission with instructing everyone on how to vote legally and transparently. Frankly, I think they were disappointed!

The election was a month away, so I told them that I'd be impartial throughout the process and would stay until my mission was completed. That mission: to bring openness and dialogue among all the major parties.

But that's not all. I also thought it would be a good idea to introduce the idea that I wasn't there merely for electoral reasons, that perhaps I could do some good elsewhere. I certainly had enough time while in country—a month in Kinshasa feels like a year elsewhere. What issue exactly I would work on I wasn't sure. So I gathered all the human-rights groups I could find and brought them together—Amnesty International, Doctors without Borders, Human Rights Watch. (I was glad they agreed to meet with me, but I was reminded of something that had irked me for a long time: For all the good work they do, they are almost all white people. Years ago I told them they should get some Hispanics in there, but what can I say—*no me escuchan*.) Still, I was more than happy to see them, because anytime you can rally the troops behind you, anytime you can build a base of support before you begin your negotiation, not only can your numbers intimidate the other side, it also lends you the confidence of knowing you're not alone. A dangerous country like the Congo can be a lonely place when all you've got is a blue blazer and a plea for peace.

Almost to a one, the NGOs agreed that in the Congo (and sadly, in too many African countries), one of the most vital and vile issues was the horrifying problem of sexual violence against women, too often used by the military to gain control of the population—to subjugate wives and girls, and to intimidate their husbands and families. It was a massive concern. It's estimated that four hundred thousand women are raped in the Congo every year. So I asked each of the NGOs what would be the most effective method to combat it. They told me that before the election, we should get each of the major political parties to commit to a promise—in writing—to fight sexual violence should they be elected. It seemed a small step, and perhaps a toothless and unenforceable one, but I was happy to do it. Any negotiation benefits from having a multifold agenda; it lets the other side know you've been thinking about their issue from many angles, and you're not just trying to strong-arm them into going along with you on a sole point. So I told my aide Mike Stratton we now had three missions: to get the parties to communicate before the election, to ensure political transparency *for* the election, and to insist on a declaration to combat violence against women from whoever *won* the election.

After I called on all the opposition presidential candidates, I still hadn't scored a meeting with Kabila. If he didn't guarantee transparency in these elections, all our work was lost. So I waited. And I waited. I then reached out to the presidential elections commissioner to see how we could work together on the issue of transparency. I also thought it might be my avenue to the president, since Daniel Ngoy Mulunda, a short, French-speaking pastor, was Kabila's man. But his allegiance also meant that, despite his being a man of the cloth and the subject of an all-seeing God, I had reason to worry: Would he care about transparency?

C'est la vie.

I was right. His initial response was noncommittal. Although I did enjoy trying out my weak French with him (my minor in the subject at Tufts was largely forgotten), and he was patient with me, speaking as slowly as I did. (Some may remember I had tried to speak French at the New Hampshire primary and it was a disaster, so this was a nice confidence builder.) We discussed the violence rampant in the country, and how I had achieved a meeting with every candidate except his implied favorite, Kabila. I was tempted to add, *And as you know, I kinda got him elected! Repay the favor!* But I wasn't sure if the joke would work in French, nor did I want to be so confrontational. He may have been a slow-talking, God-fearing, short man, but he had a big ego, and I knew he didn't want to be pilloried in the press.

A big ego. Now there's something you can negotiate toward.

On the advice of my senior official Mike Stratton, we changed our tactic and tried something that is almost a surefire winner in these kinds of situations: We appealed to Mulunda's sense of glory.

Appealing to ego is almost always an effective tactic in negotiations, even when your adversary is a pastor. But it's not about simply buttering a person up and telling them they emit only sweet odors. Anyone can do that. The key: After you do that, you have to challenge the person to live up to his or her destiny as a game changer and history maker. Contrary to the adage, flattery won't get you nowhere. Nor will it get you everywhere. But it *might* get you somewhere.

"Reverend Mulunda," I said. "You are a man of the Lord. You are a man of the people." That was my windup. "But now," I said, "you have a chance to be a hero." Every positive thing I had heard people say about him, I repeated for the next five minutes. Well, maybe three. (I hadn't heard much.)

Not surprisingly, it seemed to break the ice. He began to return the compliment (well, compliments), telling me he admired me for having a long history in the Congo and was impressed by my ability to get such good local press. He said that because of my clear devotion to his country over the years, he would call a meeting of all the political parties and announce to them what his electoral commission was willing to do to ensure fairness in the election. He didn't provide many more details than that, but my first goal was getting closer: A dialogue was beginning. I could tell from their smiles that the NGO workers were happy—and maybe a little surprised—with the progress made with just a few compliments thrown his way.

I pressed a little further on what kind of other guarantees he could offer. I had been urged by electoral experts back in the States to try to split the presidential and legislative elections as a way of defusing tensions and making their chosen representatives more directly representative, rather than a package deal. But I didn't bring it up with Mulunda right then, because one last concession on his part was already more than enough: He muttered something about allowing election monitors. That put a smile on my face as well, but just about blew the NGO workers' minds.

Enough success for one day.

Finally, he asked, "When are you leaving?"

Hmm. I had to think about my answer for a moment. I was

planning to stay through the election later in the week, naturally. But I also knew that I wanted to keep his feet to the fire, to pin him down as soon as possible, ideally within twenty-four hours—a pivotal tactic in negotiations of any kind. If your boss offers you a bigger office, start packing the boxes as soon as you get back to your old one; let her know that you're taking her seriously. So without answering directly, I merely said, "Reverend, can we do this tomorrow?" I actually thought for a moment about any scripture I might quote about God suggesting that the time for action is now, but I couldn't think of any. To this day, I do wonder if he would have noticed had I made one up.

As the Lord said in the First Epistle to the Corinthians, "Let's do this!"

Yeah, he probably would have noticed.

Still, I implied to a holy man that I was leaving earlier than I was, and I hoped that the Lord would forgive me.

I then asked politely if it would be all right if together we brought this message public, even though I knew the reverend would say yes. He wasn't the kind to shy away from the cameras, and as it says in the Gospel of Luke, *Even a reverend doesn't mind a little good press.*

So we held a joint meeting covered by the local media and announced the accord we had forged: that, thankfully, the parties would start talking for the first time, and thanks to the election monitors the election would be held with a higher degree of transparency. Of course, as proof that no good deed goes unpunished, I noticed that a few of the opposition candidates were disappointed with the promise of fair elections later that week, because they thought Kabila would win anyway, and they were secretly hoping the vote would be delayed.

Ah well.

Nonetheless, every major candidate attended the press

conference, there was massive coverage, and Mulunda made public the promise he had made privately: greater transparency.

However, I knew there was still work to be done. It was all well and good to have the election commissioner offer his guarantees, but unless President Kabila himself voiced his support for the idea of real electoral transparency, it wasn't going to happen. And that required that the president and I meet. We had tried again to set up a meeting through the US ambassador to the Congo, James Entwistle, but had no luck. (Not to embarrass James too much, but I should add that he even asked aloud, "If you get to meet with him, can I come?")

I buttered Mulunda up some more. I pointed at the cameras as they were being packed up and said, "Reverend, I did this just for you." He laughed. And he was clearly basking in the press attention. And although the press that resulted was good, no one had quite said *Richardson has pulled off a coup.* Even though it had all happened in a day—a day!—they seemed to know that Kabila wasn't yet on board, and that all I could claim so far was that I had met with everybody *except* the president.

"Reverend," I said, "I'm gonna be embarrassed if this doesn't work out."

He seemed to take a little pity on me, and said he'd work to get me in to see Kabila.

"Fine, good, great," I said. "But when you ask for the meeting, make sure he knows that I'm not here to tell him to leave the country."

"Good idea," he admitted. "Because we know you're here as a representative of Obama, and your president probably wants—"

"No," I interrupted him. "Obama may not even know about this trip." Immodestly, I have to think Obama must have known about the trip, but I thought it was important to distance myself from any official policy that might imply regime change of any sort. I was just a humble former governor trying to make sure all the votes were counted. And I needed Kabila to know that.

The next morning I got a phone call. The president was willing to meet, I was told, and even better, he was waiting for me just a few hours away.

"By car?" I asked.

"By plane," I was told. I laughed. If it's true that everything in Los Angeles is "twenty minutes away" by car, then it's equally true that everything in Africa, especially her leaders, are "a few hours away" by plane.

But as the Lord said, *Let's do this!*

So I boarded a small plane, we flew into a small village, we drove to a smaller village, we entered a very muddy tent house, and there he was: Joseph Kabila.

And after all that—the recon, the consensus building, the twisting of arms—the rest was much easier than I ever could have expected.

He was dressed in fatigues and surrounded by his guards and staff. But he said—in a surprisingly feminine voice I didn't recall—"This will just be me and the governor talking."

Admittedly, a few members of his staff stuck around, but I appreciated the gesture. And without too much trouble, he agreed to many of my requested concessions. Namely, he was willing to allow for greater transparency for the upcoming election. What's more, he signed the sexual violence statement right then and there. I even asked him to commit to attend an environmental conference to protect the forests, and he said yes. He practically pulled out a day planner and penciled it in. Frankly, I was starting to worry that he was just shining me on, and that the minute I left he would forget everything he had said.

But it was all I had, and I took it.

Then I asked, "Did your father ever talk to you about me?"

"Yes," he said. "He would often tell me you were always very stubborn."

I grinned. That's when I knew he was being entirely honest.

The election was held later that week. Kabila won a new five-year term with 48 percent of the vote, earning (or at least *getting*) three million more votes than his closest opponent. There was some fraud, to be sure, but most indications are that he would have won anyway.

Hugo Chávez:

ALÓ PRESIDENTE

I PROMISED TO TELL YOU about the handshakes.

As you can imagine, politics is a contact sport, and I've been in the handshake business for decades now. In fact, on September 16, 2002, during my first campaign for governor of New Mexico, I put President Theodore Roosevelt to shame. Handshake-wise, at least. On that day, I broke the Bull Moose's record for most handshakes given in a single eight-hour period. Whereas Roosevelt once squeezed the hands of 8,513 Americans at a White House reception in 1908, I did almost 5,000 better, shattering Teddy's record by pressing the flesh—single-handedly, if you'll forgive the pun—of 13,392 New Mexicans at a state fair.

Don't be too impressed; I wasn't in it for the glory of holding my own world record. I truly wanted to meet each and every one of those voters to establish a personal connection with them (however fleeting) and make my first gubernatorial victory as much of a landslide as possible. I wanted a mandate earned by winning by as many votes as I could wrangle, and I certainly think that day at the state fair helped give me one. Still, you have to hand it to me—that day has been cited many times as an example that I carry with me a tremendous amount of patience and stamina.

And perhaps not enough hand sanitizer.

I must say this, however. While Roosevelt couldn't match my endurance, there was one contemporary politician I came to know over the decades who certainly could. Hugo Chávez, the Venezuelan president who ruled the socialist South American country from 1999 until he died in March of 2013, could have easily lapped me, had he put his mind to it. This was a man who, only months before his death, gave a nine-and-a-half-hour speech, even after he had already battled back from a recurrence of cancer. And he did it against doctor's orders. His medical team had advised him to speak for no longer than three hours. He claims he lost track of time. I have to doubt that; after all, his sign-off—after 570 minutes of typically bombastic oratory—was the real message that day: "I'm back."

It was quite a feat, although Hugo would probably have agreed with me that a tip of the hat—and of the vocal cords—must go out to the sixty-two-year-old Catalan government worker Lluis Colet, who now holds his own Guinness record in speechifying, giving a speech that lasted five straight days and four nights in 2009. (The topic? Spanish painter Salvador Dalí. One suspects that by the end of the five days Colet himself resembled one of Dalí's more warped paintings.)

Speeches weren't Chávez's only forte. He was also a tireless broadcaster. For more than a decade, he hosted his own television talk show, *Aló Presidente*, a marathon-length weekly program extolling the many glories of Venezuela (and, of course, the many flaws of American foreign policy). More a telethon than a telecast, it would routinely last six hours.

Me? I've never even *watched* television for six hours.

With all that time spent talking, it's hard to imagine that Chávez had the hours or the energy left over to actually govern his country. Yet he did, forcefully and autocratically, ruling over Venezuela with well-documented ambition and a self-concocted political ideology known as, coincidentally enough, *Chávism*. In keeping with the tenets of Chávism—essentially his own form of socialism—during Chávez's tenure he evolved from a charismatic leader who aligned himself with the economic policies of the United States to an even more charismatic leader who was downright hostile to America and Americans. Specifically, he took special delight in lambasting Condoleezza Rice, and famously, in a speech at the General Assembly of the United Nations, once called President George W. Bush "the devil" who had left a foul smell at the same podium the day prior. "The devil came here yesterday," he said, "and it smells of sulfur still today." He then made the sign of the cross, clasped his hands in prayer, and looked up toward the heavens as if to invoke God. "Yesterday," he continued, "from this rostrum, the president of the United States, the gentleman to whom I refer to as the devil, came here, talking as if he owned the world."

It was one of Chávez's shorter speeches; of course, say something memorable like that and you don't need to talk for too long for people to remember you.

Naturally, there is one other comment from Chávez that I find memorable: Despite his general and strident anti-Americanism, he once said there was only one American politician he could truly deal with—a fellow by the name of Bill Richardson. (And with that backhanded compliment, he became yet another despot who damned me with praise. Later, during my presidential campaign, I'd often be asked, to my embarrassment, "Are you Chávez's favorite American politician?") But Chávez seemed to mean it. Throughout my first term as governor, his foreign policy team would always try to get me to visit him in Venezuela, to discuss what foreign policy issue exactly, I don't know.

Philosophically, I did think it was important to engage with Chávez, even though few politicians agreed with me. As I told Jon Lee Anderson of the *New Yorker*, "I am concerned that, because of our policy to isolate Chávez, we may have created a vacuum in Latin America. . . . Isolating him is not in our interest." I meant it. I also said, "I question whether we would be wise to brand Chávez a state sponsor of terror . . . [in light] of our energy needs."

I was just being honest.

And I had met him before. In 1999, when Chávez was the president-elect of Venezuela and I was the secretary of energy in the Clinton administration, Chávez visited DC and I was dispatched to meet him—*send the Hispanic to talk to the Hispanic* was the thinking. As a swearing-in gift, I brought him a Rawlings baseball glove, and took care to make it a left-handed pitcher's glove since I knew he was a southpaw. (Yes, a leftie in more ways than one.) It was a pleasant meeting, and when we said goodbye, I told him I'd be seeing him again at his inauguration in Caracas. He asked me, "Isn't Clinton or Gore coming?" When I told him it would just be me, he cringed a little. He wanted a heavy hitter; I was just the cabinet member who'd brought him a baseball glove. I chose to take no offense. The inauguration, held in a castle in Caracas (where Fidel and I shared a mutual nod of the head), was a splendid affair.

As my second term as governor began in 2007, I'd grown a bit restless, having become somewhat addicted to foreign policy and the foreign travel that came with it. I hadn't had an adventure in a while, except for a trip to North Korea with Wolf

Blitzer. I was feeling some diplomacy wanderlust. I had a hunch that if Chávez were to call on me again, asking me to come visit, I might just hop a flight to Caracas.

And as it happens, in 2008, I *got the call*, as they say in the game. I was summoned to South America. Although this time, the reason wasn't nearly as festive as a party in a castle. In 2003, three American men working under a contract with Northrop Grumman had been captured by the leftist Revolutionary Armed Forces of Colombia, or FARC, when their plane crashed in a rebel-controlled jungle area while on an antidrug mission. The FARC said the men—and others, including Ingrid Betancourt, the high-profile French Colombian politician they had jailed—would be released only in exchange for members of their own group who had been incarcerated by the Colombian government. Five years later, the families of the three men asked if I could meet with Chávez in Venezuela to see if he would help get them released. I didn't know if Chávez would be willing to play ball this time, but I said I would try.

A month before the trip, I had been in Bogotá to meet with Colombian president Álvaro Uribe. And although I felt I had made inroads with him on the matter, the truth is that Chávez was seen as a key player in the diplomacy surrounding the men. In fact, the FARC guerrillas had unilaterally freed six hostages to him earlier that year. So the families, who obviously had been following the cases very closely, were right to suggest a meeting with the Venezuelan president.

Still, on the day I arrived, Chávez wasn't optimistic. As my flight landed, he declared to the local press that he wasn't sure he could help: "I can't go into the Colombian jungle to rescue those people," he said. Frankly, I imagine he could have done just that had he set his mind to it, but I understood the message: *You might not get what you want.*

But he also added that he'd receive me "with pleasure" and that he hoped "the day will come when we can talk with the US establishment with respect, as equals speaking to equals." That was enough encouragement for me, since it also fell right in line with my overriding, overarching, universal theory of negotiation: It's always better to talk.

I arrived overprepared, as I always try to be no matter how high the stakes. I had already drafted at least some of what I would say after I met with Chávez, in order to ensure the best chance of enlisting his help. My precooked statement included both a placeholder for what we would (hopefully) agree on as well as wording that would publicly remind him that he'd done this exact thing—rescue hostages from the FARC—not only before, but recently, and therefore there were no excuses to be made. No punting. I would not take no for an answer.

Allow me to take a moment to emphasize the need for this kind of preparation. It's usually a good idea to predetermine the language of your diplomacy as much as possible, and to have a good sense of what you'll say and do outside the theater when the fat lady has sung and the show went either well or badly. Often there's precious little time to get your own act together before the cameras outside ask you what you thought of what went down inside.

To give you a sense of how important it is to be prepared in a negotiation, here is some of what I wrote in consultation with my advisors. Keep in mind that the following was drafted before I even met with Chávez.

> *Today, President Chávez and I had the opportunity to get reacquainted and to discuss the Acuerdo Humanitario en Colombia.*
> *As this group will remember, the FARC handed*

over six Colombian hostages to President Chávez earlier this year.

The principle of reuniting families is a principle we all can agree upon.

As such, President Chávez and I have agreed to the following.

1.

2.

3.

I believe that these actions can be the first steps—delicate, but vital steps—toward reuniting the hostages—American, French, and Colombian— with their families as quickly and safely as possible.

My point being: Arrive prepared—right down to how you'll enumerate your successes as soon as you've achieved them— and be ready to describe the importance of the agreement clearly and passionately. You can always amend your words, but you never want to be left speechless.

Chávez and I were due to meet at the Palacio de Miraflores, the presidential palace. I showed up on time; Chávez arrived several hours late. I had been running a slow boil about that, but it turned out he had come directly from pitching in a baseball game. He was still wearing cleats and his Puma gym clothes. How could I be angry about that?

Interestingly, Chávez had with him not only a stunningly beautiful Navy aide—for all I knew, she was his bat girl—but also his ambassador to the United States.

As we sat down and began to speak comfortably in Spanish, I started things off with another baseball-related peace offering, to continue the theme started at his inauguration. (Again, a thoughtful gift is *never* a bad idea.) This time I gave Hugo a baseball signed by Mickey Mantle, Willie Mays, and Duke Snider. Chávez seemed touched by the gesture, and it sparked in him a memory: He told me he had used the glove I had given him years earlier to play a friendly game in Cuba. I was glad to hear it; at least it didn't end up in his closet. Of the baseball now in his hands, he looked at the signatures closely and remarked, "Everybody knows Mantle was better than Snider." I'm always amused when leaders—Chávez and Castro as the leadoffs—not only know their baseball, but also want me *to know* they know their baseball.

Speaking of good pitching, Chávez's most important comment early in our conversation had nothing to do with his skill on the mound. And it was born of his frustration with previous attempts at diplomacy with other foreign leaders, many of whom tried to hurl insults and use invective to bully each other around. Chávez had a different plan for us: "We can talk, Richardson," he said. "We don't need to throw rocks at each other."

I couldn't agree more.

We can talk, and we should talk. It's like he was reciting my motto back to me.

Our negotiation followed the usual pattern I've experienced with foreign leaders, especially those in Latin and South America. Before getting to the matter at hand—in this case, the exfiltration of the three Americans—most want to discuss their country's treatment at the hands of United States foreign policy. When they have a representative of the United States— whether official or, in my case, unofficial—in their home, they see it as a rare opportunity to be heard directly. To shake a hand, share a meal, and air a grievance. That's okay—my theory of negotiation is that it's fine to let them vent, as long as they don't rant. Although I do admit that as Chávez began, I knew there was a chance I was in for a nine-hour speech. Thankfully he put his complaints rather simply: He was tired of being demonized by members of the Bush administration, even as they were headed for the exits from government service. He also said that he had noticed I had endorsed the candidacy of then-senator Obama, adding, "We could use better treatment from the United States."

I got the sense that he believed he had a better shot at such a new relationship with Obama than with the Republican candidate, John McCain, since Obama had said previously that he'd be willing to meet even with leaders who were hostile to the United States—namely, Iran's Mahmoud Ahmadinejad, Cuba's Castro, and yes, Venezuela's Chávez—"without precondition."

Obama believed—and as you know by now, I wholeheartedly agree—that we're almost always better off talking. You can't negotiate if you don't talk. Obama has often said when addressing hostile regimes around the world, "We will extend a hand if you unclench your fist." As someone who holds the world record for number of handshakes, obviously I agree.

So Chávez and I began to *talk*.

To be honest, it didn't start off too well. When I asked him to help negotiate with the FARC, he said something I never saw coming: "I don't know the FARC."

I had to stifle a laugh. Chávez had of course been accused for years of supplying weapons to the rebel group, and whether or not that's true (I suspect it was), for him to maintain that he "didn't know" the FARC—*FARC who?*—was a silly thing to say. At the very least, he must have remembered when the FARC had released six hostages to him just a few months prior. That's the kind of thing that sticks with you.

I more or less overlooked his evasion and plodded on.

"Presidente, I come to you with three simple requests."

"We shall see how simple they are," he said.

"*Por supuesto,*" I said. Of course.

"Presidente, I ask you three things. First, that although I am not here as a representative of the United States government, you officially accept me as someone who can help us navigate this problem. I would like to be a key mediator in this situation."

This seemed easy enough, but it was an important step. He had to explicitly recognize me as his equal in this negotiation, even though by all indications this was the case. After all, I was talking directly to the president of Venezuela, so that suggests a certain equal status. Any negotiation—big or small—should, to the extent possible, be between equal parties who have equal power to say yes or no. And I needed him to grant me that status publicly, in front of our staffs. These things can't be implied; they must be explicit.

Say you're meeting with the boss—perhaps not of a country, but of your company. Even though he or she *is* your boss, and has more power at the office than you do generally, in any *individual* negotiation—over a raise, say—you both have equal power to say yes or no to the terms on the table. He or she can't make you accept what's being offered. It's just as much your decision as it is their prerogative to make an offer acceptable to you. It's vital to remember that.

Why? Assuming you have higher status—which is assuming the other person is by definition inferior to you—almost always leads to bad outcomes. Maybe not today, but someday soon. Say your daughter is asking to borrow the car to go out on a Friday night. It's all too easy to say, "No, because

I'm the boss and I say so." How long will she respect that if she doesn't feel you're respecting her as an individual—one with free will and an official, hard-earned driver's license? You may have achieved the result you want this time around, but you've likely blown up any future negotiations. Next time, since she knows you're being unilateral and autocratic (although she might use very different adjectives), she may just take the keys when you're not looking.

Anyhow, Chávez assented, and I moved on.

"Second, I ask that you get involved in this situation yourself. That you help on the matter of rescuing these hostages and delivering them back to American custody."

On this matter, he said nothing. It was the only chance we had of getting the hostages returned, so I was truly hoping he'd assent quickly. But he remained silent.

I had no choice but to continue. My third favor, as I had planned it on my trip down, was going to be merely that he acknowledge that the entire United States government—not just the lone governor sitting across from him—also wanted him to get involved in the rescue. But at this point, as we sat there in silence without his agreement to get involved, my third request didn't seem strong enough.

So I improvised.

"And finally," I said, not sure where the idea was coming from, "finally, Presidente, I ask that you help me get in touch with the FARC."

I asked politely. I respected his authority. I threw no stones.

But I didn't mean a word I said.

The lesson: When you have no cards, invent some! As long as you're willing to do what you say—I didn't *want* to visit the FARC, but I would if Chávez pointed me toward them—it's okay to throw a new wrench into the proceedings.

Chávez looked at his advisors, and then back to me. "Señor Richardson."

I wasn't at all sure what he was going to say next.

"You want to see the FARC?" he asked.

"If that's what it takes," I said. I didn't really want to see the FARC, but I wanted him to *think* I wanted to see the FARC. That I was at least willing to do something bold and brash, because the return of the hostages was that important to me. "I need to see these hostages returned. So either you go get them yourself, or let me do it."

Chávez laughed.

"Although," I continued, "I'm not sure what I'm going to give them in return. A *baseball*?!"

Chávez laughed harder.

"Maybe we can play a game right there in the jungle. Clear out the trees, and put down a diamond."

Now even my staff was laughing.

"Señor Richardson! Understand me, please," he said. "I would not suggest that you go into the jungle. Your security would be at risk."

Trust me, I know. That's why I want you to do it.

"As you know, the FARC doesn't meet in a camp, or under a tent, or in a building," he said. "They meet in a cave. They are always around danger. If they turn on a radio, within thirty minutes comes a bomb. I tell you this because what you're asking is too difficult."

You don't need to tell me this.

Chávez then looked at his advisors, gave the smallest of nods, then turned back to me. After a few moments of silence, he spoke up.

"We need some time," he said.

Time to do what?

"I will send a message to FARC. Through someone else."

That's what I was waiting for.

"*Gracias*, Presidente," I said.

"I will send a message, and we will see if it arrives," he added.

"*Gracias*, Presidente," I said again.

"You see," he said, leveling with me, "I am not in agreement in the holding of civilians. People being in jails like pigs? This is not humane. In jail, people deserve medicine. Soldiers are prisoners of war. But civilians? No."

"I agree, Presidente."

"But, Señor Richardson?"

"Yes?"

"These civilians. Are they CIA?"

I was honest. "I don't think so, Presidente. I have met the families. One of the grandmothers is Colombian."

This seemed to animate Chávez.

"Okay, okay," he said. "*Sí, te ayudo.*"

I will help you.

We had started to wrap up the meeting when Chávez was moved to tell me one more thing.

"Bill," he said. "I need to tell you something. I want you to know something."

"*¿Sí?*"

"I have a secret plan I've never told anyone about. Can you keep a secret?"

"I can keep one of yours," I told him.

He leaned in close, but said it loudly enough for everyone to hear. Clearly this was a secret he wanted everyone to know about.

"This is my secret," he said. "I am going to buy the Yankees!" he said with a huge laugh.

Everyone else laughed.

"Great," I said. "But first, help me get these hostages out."

He nodded. He seemed willing.

Then, of course, we shook on it.

As I left the presidential palace, I was mobbed by a throng of reporters. I was happy to share the news. "President Chávez has agreed to try and help," I said. "He told me '*Sí, te ayudo.*'" Later, long after I had returned to New Mexico, I was told by other Venezuelan officials that Chávez did in fact try to help. Whether he played an instrumental role, I still don't know for sure. All I know for certain is that the three hostages were eventually rescued by the Colombian military and went home to their wives and families.

Considering the stamina Chávez had, it's hard to believe he would ever pass away. And for a time, even after press reports gave accounts of his death on March 5, 2013, some Venezuelans honestly believed he hadn't. But on that day, after a long struggle with cancer and a last-ditch attempt at treatment in Cuba, the word was out: Chávez was no more.

El presidente había muerto.

A month later, I received a call from José Miguel Insulza, the secretary general of the Organization of American States (OAS).

"I'd like you to go to Venezuela," he told me.

"Why?" I asked him. *After all,* I thought to myself, *it's not like I can negotiate with Chávez any longer.*

Insulza explained that the election to replace Chávez could boil over if it wasn't seen throughout the election process as legitimate. It was a tight and tightening race between two popular Venezuelan politicians: former bus driver Nicolás Maduro Moros, Chávez's foreign minister, right-hand man, and chosen successor; and conservative Henrique Capriles Radonski, the charismatic but bellicose governor of Miranda and former mayor of Baruta who once spent four months in jail for protesting Chávez outside the Cuban Embassy—before being reelected mayor with 80 percent of the vote.

Admittedly, the election was getting a little heated, and frankly a bit strange. Even though Maduro had been handpicked by Chávez publicly and directly, he seemed intent on reinforcing that impression to an absurd degree, even to those supporters who didn't need convincing. At rallies, he would invoke Chávez in almost every sentence. And although that might be expected of any candidate in his position, Maduro went further. He insisted on one television program that after Chávez's death, the former Venezuelan president had flown to him as a small bird and announced that Maduro would emerge victorious—Chávez's ghost's version of tweeting his support, I suppose. At rallies, Maduro would introduce to the crowd a small man who was, eerily, the spitting image of the former supreme *comandante*. And—this was my favorite— Maduro insisted that an ancient tribal curse would befall anyone who dared vote for Capriles. Even those without the threat of a curse had to suffer through Maduro as he rapped— yes, *rapped*—about the spirit of Chávez lingering among the assembled crowd.

For this reason and others—including some far more consequential, such as the need for political transparency, the fear of electoral corruption, and the threat of pre- and postelection violence—Insulza was solicitous and clear: "We'd like you to keep an eye on the election," he told me. "As our representative."

Having developed a vested interest in the future of the

country thanks to my visits with Chávez, I happily complied. So I once again flew to Caracas, accompanied this time by the chief of staff of the OAS.

I didn't expect that I'd need to negotiate my way into meetings with both candidates—the stakes were high for both men—yet by the time I arrived only Maduro seemed willing to meet. When we arrived at the presidential palace, Maduro was already there. We greeted each other as friends, having spent some important time together four years earlier while negotiating the release of the FARC prisoners. Hitting the campaign trail evidently had interrupted his exercise routine, and he had packed on several pounds.

We were soon joined by seven other diplomats—delegates from Panama, the Dominican Republic, and Uruguay; a former representative of Mexico; and officials from other Latino countries. There had been barely any time for pleasantries when Maduro indicated what so many had come to know—that he was intent on proving that, as the front-runner, he was "Chávez's ghost." And he did so in the only way he could in such a situation: He launched into a speech. Thankfully, his oratory on this day was a merciful forty-five minutes. Perhaps he was saving his nine-hour speeches for after he was elected. As president, he promised to follow the legacy of Chávez and continue to fulfill his dream of creating a paradise of unbridled Chávism in Venezuela. Amusingly, he ordered—not requested, but ordered—the assembled media to cover his speech in full.

One particular detail in his speech alarmed me, considering where my flight had originated that day. He insisted that the United States was complicit in Chávez's death. Namely, that the United States had poisoned him.

After describing the details of what could only be considered a ludicrous conspiracy, he asked us if we had any questions.

Yeah, I do, I thought. *Where the hell did you get that idea?* Anyhow, that's the question I wanted to ask. But I raised my hand with another.

"Mr. Foreign Minister," I asked, "how are you going to treat the Organization of American States and the United States if you should be elected?"

I was there as a representative of the OAS, not to represent the United States. But to be honest, I thought, *Screw it. He's accusing America of killing his predecessor.* Invoking the United States might get a more interesting response. I expected a general answer—something diplomatic and noncommittal—but he got surprisingly specific. And, frankly, personal.

"Well, Governor Richardson. As you know, you have been a friend to Venezuela. Not the US. But *you.* You are our friend."

Oh great. Yet another wannabe strongman telling me how good I am to him. Just what I need: more wall space in the Dictator Hall of Fame!

"You have always treated Venezuela with respect," he said.

This is where I expected him to say, "But *America,* on the other hand . . . "

Instead he surprised me.

"All I want is for America to treat us the same way," he said. "I want to regularize our relationship with the US. And I see no reason we can't do that."

You mean the fact that you think we killed your boss and mentor isn't going to be a problem for you?

"As for the OAS," he continued, "tell the secretary general we will stay put. We will continue to be a member, if he gives us his word he will do his best to reform it so we feel like an equal partner in the organization."

I have to say, I was shocked. And as I half-listened to the other delegates ask a series of softball questions, I thought of his reasonable answer to my question and thought, *Well, at least now we're getting somewhere.*

If only his opponent Capriles would be so willing to talk.

As the conference began to break up, I was told by one of Maduro's aides that he'd like to have a private word with me. I was waiting to find out which room we'd retire to when the aide urged me on. "Just walk around the table," he said.

I thought you said private.

So I walked around to Maduro's side of the table and leaned in.

"Governor Richardson," Maduro whispered.

"Yes?" I said.

"You were always a good friend to the supreme *comandante*"—by which he meant his departed boss, Hugo Chávez. "In fact, whenever you visited him, you gave him a gift."

Uh-oh. This guy's probably wondering why I didn't bring a gift for him too. And I hadn't. My mistake.

"You gave him a baseball with the signature of Mickey Mantle."

Here it comes, I thought. *He's about to ask for one of his own, and I arrived empty-handed.*

Instead, Maduro's face fell and he looked sheepish and guilty.

"And Governor Richardson," he said. "I must tell you: We can't find it."

Thank heaven. I thought I had offended. I laughed and immediately reassured Maduro that that was perfectly acceptable. What's more, if he wanted another, I said I was sure I could find one for him.

Then he got back to business. "I meant what I said," he said. "I want you to send a message to the United States that I want to regularize our relationship and exchange ambassadors as soon as possible."

Part of me wondered if I could somehow get Mickey Mantle's ghost to help out.

He continued: "I'd like you to meet with our foreign minister tomorrow. Elías Jaua Milano. I'll let him know you're coming." Frankly, I thought that, technically, Maduro was still acting president. Clearly he was planning for permanent victory.

After I left the event, I reported what Maduro had said to our highest-ranking State Department official in Venezuala, who told me he passed the information on to Washington. Then I set out to get the other half of what I had come for: a meeting with Henrique Capriles.

Despite coming on very strong as the election approached, Capriles was proving to be very reluctant to meet with anyone, let alone a representative of the OAS intent on making sure the election was fair. Perhaps in his mind, he needed to devote all of his attention to campaigning. Or perhaps he thought everyone not in his orbit had sold out. Whatever the reason, he was untouchable and unreachable.

Instead, we arranged a meeting with two of his top campaign aides. But rather than try to negotiate the terms of their campaign's participation in a free and fair election with them, I told them what a mistake it was to keep their candidate at arm's length.

"This isn't just a local election," I told them. "I don't know how much you realize it, but the world is watching. This is an international election, and the international community is going to judge you—win or lose."

They seemed not to connect the dots.

"Look, if your candidate wins, but you haven't made him available to me—or to anyone else, for that matter—there will always be questions about whether he deserved to win. It's in your best interest to at least introduce me to him."

They sat there silently.

"Well, I've said my piece," I said.

I gave up, I got up, and I left. Sometimes the best move you can make in a negotiation is the one that takes you out of the room. I had no idea if I'd ever meet Capriles, let alone help the OAS sanction either his victory or his defeat. But I had made every effort I could muster to try to meet with him. Now it was up to him.

With nothing left to lose—or, frankly, to do—I decided to spend election morning shuttling between polling places in Caracas to get a feel for how things were developing. And frankly, my impression for most of the day was that there was very little excitement about front-runner Maduro. Most of the electricity seemed to be charging toward Capriles. On Maduro's side of the fence, there was very little intensity. If I had had to guess, I would have said Capriles was on the road to victory—all the more reason to meet with whoever could help make his victory legitimate.

At noon I met with the foreign minister, Elías Jaua. He was wearing workout clothes, despite there being no appearance of having actually worked out. (I've often wondered if I should adopt that look; people presume you're always coming from the gym, even if you came from a buffet. Can't hurt, right?) As directed by his boss, Jaua continued the conversation I had begun with Maduro. His deal points were clear: If the United

States was willing to regularize the Venezuela–US relationship, Venezuela would open up the taps and sell the States more oil, Venezuela would cooperate more fully on drug enforcement, and Venezuela and the United States could exchange ambassadors ("You name one, we'll name one").

I took a moment to recognize what had happened in just twenty-four hours. I was thrilled that what had begun as a trip to encourage a legitimate election had transformed into a bona fide diplomatic mission. Often trips like this fall apart. Rare is the one that gets even more ambitious.

Before I could revel in the development, I got a call from my handler from the OAS.

"He'll meet."

Who? I had almost forgotten.

"Capriles. He'll meet."

I had to assume that he, too, smelled the scent of victory.

It was midafternoon and the polls would close in a few hours, so we rushed over to meet with the candidate in a voting area filled with Capriles aficionados. His people. The scene was chaotic. Supporters shouted. Horns honked.

They first took me to meet Capriles's family, who thoughtfully served me and my traveling companions arepas, traditional Venezuelan sandwiches of various meats, sharp cheeses, and black beans. I'm not easily swayed by such gestures, but I have to admit they were delicious. We ate and enjoyed watching the frantic madness around us, although we were still anxious to meet with the MIA candidate. From what I could tell, Capriles still hadn't arrived. Finally I inquired about his whereabouts.

"Oh, he's here," his brother told us. "He was just waiting for you to finish your sandwich!"

What? I flew here to see him, not eat a sandwich!

(Although, again, damn good sandwich.) I made a show of wiping my lips with my napkin and made it clear to Capriles's brother what was next on the menu. Time to meet.

Finally, Capriles arrived. And—perhaps only so as not to alarm me—he too was wearing workout clothes. (American politicians wear a suit and tie on Election Day; perhaps they're not sweating enough!) Surprisingly, despite the surging supporters and the honking horns and the optimistic polling, Capriles didn't feel the confidence I thought he would.

"I worry," he told me.

"You don't think you can win?" I asked him. "I think you can win."

"No, I won't win," he told me. "There's too much cheating. And the students will vote now. It is the afternoon, and they will vote now. And they will cheat," he said. "They will vote for Maduro, because I am a conservative. Just because I am a conservative, they will cheat against me."

For an hour, we discussed the finer details of Venezuelan polling security, and the electoral proclivities of the average Venezuelan student. Capriles was not optimistic. I reminded him that it was important he stay accessible to organizations like the OAS, since if he were to win—and again I told him it was possible—it needed to be seen as legitimate. For his sake, and for his country's sake.

Finally, I bid him adios, and I asked my Venezuelan government handlers to take me to where they were tallying the election results. The polls closed, and yet—unlike the breathless coverage we've come to expect from American television networks—they announced no results. Eight p.m. Nine p.m. Still nothing. Everyone was just sitting around, ready to celebrate or commiserate. But no word. Ten p.m. Eleven p.m.

Finally, around midnight, the head of the election

commission appeared on television screens around the country. But this particular telecast did not last six hours, as Chávez's *Aló Presidente* so often would. Instead, she made a brief announcement:

Nicolás Maduro has won the election, with a scant 1 percent victory.

As the night turned into day, Capriles insisted the election had been stolen.

In turn, Maduro went on the air and claimed to be the son of Chávez.

You know, they both might have been right.

Russia:

AN IMBALANCE OF POWER

Were they kidding?

For anyone born during or after—or who has ever heard of—the Cold War, it was almost impossible to believe. Russia, historically one of the world's preeminent superpowers, a renowned master of the high-stakes international espionage game, had redeployed in its arsenal one of the world's lowest-tech communication devices: *typewriters*. And not in a time long, long ago. The year was 2013, and the headline in the July 11 *USA Today* edition made their rationale plain:

Spooked by NSA, Russia Reverts to Paper Documents

Move over, ICBMs. Hello, IBM Selectrics.

According to one source within Russia's Federal Guard Service, who chose to remain anonymous—perhaps for fear of being teased—Russia had gone back to the future for a host of reasons. "After the scandal with the spread of secret documents by WikiLeaks, the revelations of Edward Snowden, reports of listening to Dmitry Medvedev during his visit to the G20 summit in London, the practice of creating paper documents will increase." And not only *will* it increase, it *did*. By midsummer, Mother Russia had ordered twenty shiny electric typewriters.

Cloaks and daggers had been replaced by black ribbons and feed rollers.

In other words: Not exactly weaqpons of mass dis destruction.

I kid. But to be fair, the Russians were right to be on high alert. Thanks to a series of embarrassing revelations about the covert operations of the National Security Agency, America's top intelligence-gathering agency, they'd seen how secret things had hardly remained secret at all. After all, they had self-appointed NSA whistleblower/leaker Snowden hiding away in their very own Sheremetyevo airport at the time—and later granted him temporary asylum. With each revelation, the message from America to Moscow, to the world, and—disturbing many—to its own citizens was becoming crystal clear: *We know what you're up to.*

It shocked many, but honestly none of this was a surprise to me. As ambassador to the UN, and later as secretary of energy in the Clinton administration, top secrets, security clearances, high-stakes espionage, and the everyday operations of the National Security Agency turned out to be a huge part of my job. All of that experience has helped shape my approach to a serious aspect of negotiation. To a shocking extent, some might say, but I'll let you be the judge as you read this chapter.

What I'm talking about here is something called *asymmetric information*. Or, put plainly, information you have in your possession that your negotiating partner doesn't have—and doesn't know you have. And it could shape the results of that negotiation. The sticky aspect of asymmetric info lies in how you come by the information and how you feel, personally, about whether you should use it. Because, you see, at some point during some ongoing discussion with that person on the other side of the table, you might ask yourself, "Should I be doing this?"

I answered that question for myself quite easily, as you'll see. Maybe it will be that easy for you. Then again, maybe it won't.

"I need you, Billy."

The voice was President Clinton's, and the sentiment was familiar. He was going through another of the many tough episodes during his time in the presidency—it was 1998, and the Monica Lewinsky scandal was roiling—but this time his entreaty was about more than wanting my shoulder to lean on. He needed me not merely for a sympathetic ear, but for a higher calling: He wanted me to leave my beloved position as the United States ambassador to the United Nations.

"Why?" I asked.

"Peña is leaving me," he said, referring to Federico Peña, who was about to announce his departure from the position he had taken just a year before, secretary of energy. "So I need you, Billy."

"You need me to do what exactly?" I asked, although I could have guessed the answer.

"I need a Hispanic in my cabinet," he said.

It's true; he did. Bill Clinton had run for president on a promise to have a cabinet that "looks like America," and frankly he was running out of people who looked like me.

"Besides," he added, "I'd like to have my friends around right now." Ah yes, Lewinsky. I was more than familiar with what he was alluding to. Throughout that scandal, I had done my part. In private I had stayed up on many late-night phone calls offering consolation and advice as Bill navigated his way through it. In public I defended my president at length on television, to the point where I was often accused of being his lapdog. It wasn't a comfortable position, but I chose it.

So as a friend—and at that time I certainly still considered myself his friend—I wanted to help. As a proud American, I also wanted to help my president. But there was only one problem: I loved my job as UN ambassador. I had only been at the United Nations a little more than a year and felt I was just starting to thrive in what was, and is, an important position. I was doing intriguing work, addressing some of the globe's most treacherous and intractable troubles, and meeting and greeting a cast of international characters who made each day memorable. My wife, Barbara, loved it as well. We lived at the Waldorf on Park Avenue, hosted dignitaries from around the world, and made sure to take full advantage of all New York had to offer.

The job was a delightful mix of business and pleasure, even during a difficult time in international diplomacy. Iraq was starting to rear its head yet again, and my old shoe buddy (sole-mate?) Saddam Hussein, who threatened to pursue nuclear weapons in violation of a United Nations decree, demanded much of the attention of the UN Security Council. Of course I expected Saddam to stir up trouble; what I hadn't expected was the unhelpfulness of some of my fellow ambassadors at the

United Nations. I found some of the UN ambassadors eager to thwart my attempts to spur initiatives to contain not only Iraq, but also resolutions addressing Bosnia and Africa. As allies, I needed two highly skilled diplomats—sticklers for detail and whizzes at UN procedure—but the French ambassador, Alain Dejammet, and the British ambassador, John Weston, were by-the-book bureaucrats who I, ever the unconventional ambassador, knew I would need to court if I expected to get anything accomplished during my tenure.

Fortunately, I made headway with Dejammet thanks to the help of our common host: New York City itself. When the United Nations building proved too claustrophobic, I would often head to the Big Apple's famed Central Park for a long walk and a good cigar. As it happened, Dejammet was an avid photographer who would often hit the park as well, hunting for the perfect snapshot. At least that became our excuse. Occasionally we would intentionally bump into each other there, where we could speak candidly without staff or reporters, talking shop far from UN headquarters. He became an ally.

It's something to remember: When the everyday confines and formality of your workplace stymie a negotiation, removing yourselves to a remote—or at least uncommon—locale might be the ideal way to shake things up. It's why so many international treaties are struck in places like Maryland's Camp David and Wye River Plantation or even in Reykjavík, Iceland, rather than in the cramped East Room of the White House or inside the towering redbrick walls of the Kremlin. Remove the key players from their usual process, and you increase the chance for progress. It focuses the mind. I sometimes wonder if the best way to improve United States–North Korea relations would be to send President Obama and Kim Jong-un up to the International Space Station for a long weekend.

Surely then they'd have to talk. (If that ever happens, you read it here first.)

Early in my tenure at the UN, when I needed the Security Council ambassadors' help drafting a resolution condemning Iraq for its pursuit of weapons of mass destruction—a significant obligation of the Security Council during my time there—Dejammet proved vital. But even that simple, purely descriptive word—*condemn*—was something the British ambassador Weston couldn't swallow. Although my walking companion Dejammet supported me, Weston took issue with my word choice. Frankly, I had wanted something even more punitive—"strongly condemn"—but the Russian ambassador, Sergey Lavrov (now Russia's foreign minister), took issue with the adverb *strongly.*

At this point, I will pause for a reality check. Yes, diplomatic negotiations hinge on tiny little words like that. It may seem trivial or even silly to outside observers. And I grant that it's these kinds of halting debates that bestow upon the UN its occasional and regrettable—*strongly* regrettable, if you ask me—do-nothing reputation. Still, sometimes negotiation is all about the little words, the little concessions that have big meaning to some people. Attorneys are highly trained in this area (ask anyone you know who's gotten a divorce). Ultimately, as is the case with most United Nations activity, we compromised. *Strongly* was out, but *condemn* stayed in.

Another important task that came with the job was to address a chill that had descended on the United Nations when I arrived in 1997. By then, the mood in the building had cratered, thanks to everything from deep international disagreements, to the failure of the United States to pay the dues it owed the UN, to the crackdown on Russian ambassadors who had been using diplomatic immunity to void parking tickets. I knew I needed to do everything I could to boost morale. To that end, I once brought an entire delegation of the Security Council—Dejammet and Lavrov included—to a Yankees–Mets game. I insisted on giving my cohorts the full New York baseball experience: I handed out baseball caps (evenly divided between the Yankees and the Mets, of course), we downed more than our share of hot dogs and beer, and I pretended not to be disappointed when the Russian and Chinese ambassadors left before the seventh-inning stretch. (I'll give them the benefit of the doubt: Perhaps it was their attempt to behave like average Mets fans.)

Field trips to baseball games, come-one-come-all cigar breaks in the UN lounge, impromptu bull sessions with low-level UN staffers in the cafeteria—there's no denying I took an unconventional approach to the gig. By the end of my time as ambassador, even the *New York Times* reported that my diplomatic methods were "zany by United Nations standards." I was proud of that distinction, and remain so; my unconventional diplomacy, and the willingness of my fellow Security Council members to indulge it, was much of the reason I was so happy in the job.

I didn't want it to end so soon. So when Clinton asked me to join his cabinet, I thought maybe I had one ace up my sleeve. Although UN ambassador is not technically a cabinet-level position, it is often afforded cabinet-level status depending on the event, the players involved, and, frankly, the mere need to elevate its importance when convenient. So, desperate, I tried this angle.

"Bill, in a sense I already am in your cabinet!"

"Not really," he said, accurately.

"But pretty close, right?" I joked.

He laughed. "Not close enough. I need you close, Billy."

I suppose I wasn't entirely forthcoming earlier when I said the only problem I saw with joining the president's cabinet was that I loved my job at the UN. There was another pressing concern that had to do with the job Clinton was asking me to take.

"But Bill," I said, sheepishly, "I gotta be honest. I don't have much experience in energy."

Again, Bill laughed.

"That won't be a problem," he said, with the confidence of a president. And you know what? In the end, you don't negotiate with the president. You just follow.

Within a few weeks, I was the country's ninth secretary of energy.

My time leading the Department of Energy was a rollicking one, marked as much by strange experiences and difficult negotiations as unexpected controversy. Among the many unique events in my time there: After a twenty-three-course diplomatic meal in Ashgabat that featured just as many toasts of vodka, I was offered a horse by the inebriated president of Turkmenistan (I politely declined); I went toe-to-toe with a very stubborn—and very drunk—Boris Yeltsin (I politely pretended not to notice the latter); with the blessing of Ukrainian president Leonid Kuchma, I visited Chernobyl, the site of the world's worst nuclear accident, and the nearby ghost city of Pripyat to ensure that Chernobyl's reactors were shut down safely and quickly (I politely pretended not to be alarmed for my health); and in a Siberian hot spring—hardly your typical conference room—I hammered out an agreement with the Russian naval minister to work together with the Russian navy to secure nuclear weapons on Soviet ships.

Memorable experiences, all. But through all that, my experiences in both jobs—as UN ambassador and secretary of energy—really shaped my philosophy on asymmetric information because I got to see firsthand how different people with different motivations used info they had at their disposal whether they acquired it via questionable means or not.

Example: When I took the post at DOE, a nuclear scientist named Wen Ho Lee was a mechanical engineer in the so-called "X Division" at the Los Alamos National Laboratory, the renowned weapons-research facility in my home state of New Mexico. To this day, I'm fairly certain that anyone who recalls my time at the department will also quickly remember the scandal surrounding Lee's termination and the accusations that I, along with others, overreached in the investigation, detainment, and punishment of Lee, one of our chief nuclear scientists. Whether they also recollect the other salient facts of the situation I had inherited—that President Clinton had issued a presidential directive earlier that year ordering national research labs to improve security, that China had recently revealed that it knew top secret details about one of our newest warheads, that the X Division where Lee worked was tasked with developing the mathematical formulas for nuclear weapons known as the "legacy codes," that an FBI investigation called Operation Kindred Spirit had identified Lee as the most likely culprit, and that Lee had previously lied to the FBI—well, there's not much I can do about that now.

Full disclosure: I admit that I have a particular distaste for anyone who violates the trust our country puts in our security agencies. Having seen firsthand the commitment and important work of our intelligence analysts—often done in the shadows, for scant applause and low pay—I feel that those who undermine their work and our nation's security deserve the punishment they receive. My aversion to this behavior grew stronger after 9/11 and is most acute when concerning the National Security Agency, often our first and last line of defensive counterintelligence against those who wish to do us harm. Which is why I have little sympathy for those, such as Julian Assange or Bradley Manning or Edward Snowden, who take it upon themselves to expose—whatever that might mean, however they choose to define it—the necessarily closely held practices and methods of our covert operations, rather than go through the appropriate channels available to whistleblowers. Snowden and Manning were accused—and in Manning's case, found guilty—of mishandling sensitive asymmetric information because they personally believed such information should be public. It's a shame they didn't ask my advice. They wouldn't have had to shack up in a foreign embassy, or seek refuge in Russia, or be convicted of twenty criminal counts and face a lifetime in prison.

Of course I recognize this is not a black-and-white issue. But do I think self-appointed martyrs should grant themselves the authority to determine which of those methods are acceptable? I do not. When an individual's self-promotion of transparency-above-all butts up against our country's need for security, I side with our country. Simple as that.

Now, having said that, you might be wondering, maybe even slightly cynically, "Governor, what's your philosophy on using asymmetric information that *you* have?"

I'm glad you asked.

At the UN, one of the requirements of the Security Council was to schedule votes at times when the greatest number of ambassadors would be available. Or so went the theory. In reality, UN ambassadors are human and would indulge the human tendency to try to game the system. Historically, many in my position had calculated when only those ambassadors who agreed with them on a particular pressing matter could show up. I had a particularly good track record on this, for one highly amusing reason: Somehow I always knew when one highly opinionated and anti-American ambassador would be unavailable.

Specifically, when he would be visiting his mistress.

It was a perfect, seemingly foolproof gambit. I knew that anyone willing to have a mistress wasn't likely to cancel on that mistress for something as mundane as a vote, international peace be damned. Hell hath no fury like a mistress scorned.

He might have gotten wise to our shenanigans—he *had* to see the pattern—but his behavior didn't reflect that. Every time his guard went down, my batting average went up. Like clockwork, he'd feel a little amorous, and magically our voting day would get busier.

Naturally, my fellow ambassadors wondered exactly how I determined, with such certainty, that this particular ambassador would be attending to other business, if you will; I never told.

So how, then, *did* I know? Well, let's say I just did. And the information I received was *Foreign Affairs* meets *Fifty Shades of Grey*.

On my perch, where I was doing everything I could to protect American security rather than jeopardize it, the information sent my way helped me do my job better, and I made no bones about doing so.

Now here's where your own philosophy on the use of asymmetric information comes into the picture. If you believe in fair play and using straightforward negotiating tactics, you're likely to feel I overreached. If you believe that gaining and using inside info *is* fair play, you'll probably support my technique.

And that, of course, makes this a very interesting negotiation lesson to consider. At some point, whether you seek it out or "a little birdie" tells you, you'll have info in your possession that qualifies in your world as top secret. Is it always appropriate to be so cunning and calculated? It's one thing to use every trick in the book to keep a country as secure as possible. It's another to use intelligence to tilt the scales when national security isn't at stake, and I admit that not all the votes we took in the ambassador's absence were matters of life and death. And it's still quite another to bring such techniques home to negotiations with, say, your spouse.

At that level, there are two questions to consider:

One, is it smart to capitalize on asymmetric information?

And two, are you justified in gathering that information by any means necessary?

The answers? Yes and no.

Every negotiation rests upon asymmetric information. Unlike a trial in a court of law, there is no "discovery phase," no preordained time when everyone is entitled to learn anything the other side knows simply by asking. Therefore, all negotiations are unbalanced. We can only enter a room hoping that we are the smartest person in it, that we know at least marginally more than the person across from us, so we can outwit and outlast them. I'd guess that in a corporate environment, ninety-nine times out of a hundred, people would gladly—and guiltlessly—use such information to their advantage. And I'd agree that ethically, morally, there is nothing wrong with exploiting information you have, as long as it's not ill-gotten. As they say, all's fair in love and war, right?

Well, not *all*.

There are exceptions. For starters, does the benefit of having asymmetric information mean you should spy on your husband, your wife, or your children? Or if you're negotiating a raise with your boss, should you try to learn when he'll be dallying with his mistress so you can snoop on his office computer and learn the salaries of your coworkers?

Of course not. Our obligation to be ethical and moral participants in these fundamental relationships demands an obvious no. You are not America, and your spouse is not Russia. You live and work with these people.

This may seem obvious, but to some it's not. Many parents would argue that if you can get your hands on your child's Facebook password, you should have at it. The world is dangerous, they insist, and if you can protect your children from predators—by any means necessary—they'll do exactly that. I can respect their parental prerogative, but ethically and morally, that's absurd. We all deserve a zone of privacy, even when Mommy and Daddy are paying the Internet bill.

But there's a far more practical consideration. In cases like these, in the home and at the office, we don't have an NSA at our disposal. Any intel you acquired would be a product of your own duplicity. And frankly, if your spouse were ever to learn that you spied on them, it would cause resentment with repercussions far greater than the limited proportional advantage you might get with the information gained. Simply put, it's not worth the risk.

So that, to me, is the distinction. When the stakes are high, go ahead and try to learn their secrets. But when the stakes are low, or you're married to one of the stakeholders, you'll just have to gamble with the limited information you have. (Come to think of it, maybe it would be nice if somehow we could establish an NSA for Average Joes—a covert organization that would provide priceless intelligence about all the people in our lives, making us feel confident that we were just as informed as our counterparts even though we feared that we weren't. Call it the NIA: the National Insecurity Agency.)

Until the world changes for the better, let's just say that I don't blame Russia for buying those typewriters.

President
Barack Obama:
A HARD SELL VS. A SOFT TOUCH

"KATRINA."

The voice was barely a whisper, just quiet enough not to be heard by the dozen microphones surrounding us.

Pardon?

"Katrina. He's asking you about Katrina."

It was Senator Barack Obama's voice, his whisper, and it was aimed, subtly but firmly, at me.

I had just given an answer to a separate question—in this, our seemingly seven hundredth Democratic debate of the 2008 presidential campaign—and I thought the moderator had moved on down the line to grill other candidates. I assumed I had a break. To be even more honest, I had stopped listening. (If you think debates are exhausting to watch, consider how exhausting they are to participate in; you can't blame a guy for taking a mental recess or two.) Yet the fact remained: The next question had been put to me, and I hadn't even heard it.

It was a debate nightmare.

In front of millions of people.

Millions of people who I wanted to vote for me.

Me, the guy who couldn't even answer a simple question.

A simple question about . . . what again?

Oh yeah, *Katrina.*

Or at least it *could* have been a nightmare, had I not been standing next to Senator Obama. And it *would* have been, had Senator Obama—who had heard the question as clearly as he had seen that I wasn't remotely paying attention—not chosen to rescue me:

"He's asking you about Katrina."

Admittedly, I didn't know *what* the moderator was asking me about Katrina, but Obama's heads-up was enough for me to land on an answer at least somehow related to the topic.

In the cutthroat, high-stakes arena of presidential politics, the freshman senator from Illinois had had every reason to let me hang there, embarrassing myself. Most politicians would. Many politicians have.

Instead, he saw a fellow public servant about to make a face-plant on national television, and he caught me before I fell. It was a moment indicative of Senator Obama's style. Not only was he a candidate for president, he was also a gentleman.

And it was only one of many reasons why I endured one of the longest negotiations—leading to one of the most controversial decisions—of my career: endorsing Barack Hussein Obama for president in 2008.

I first met Barack Obama at the same time so many Americans first became familiar with him: the 2004 Democratic convention in Boston. Obama had been invited by Senator John Kerry to give the keynote at that year's nominating convention, an introductory speech by "a skinny kid with a funny name" that still echoes to this day.

"You gotta see this guy," Tom Daschle told me. "You gotta make sure you see this guy." As senator from South Dakota, Tom had benefited from Obama's fund-raising help in 2004, and although Tom didn't win reelection, many of his staff had joined Obama's campaign, including Obama's chief of staff, Pete Rouse. Tom was one of the first to experience Obama in action, and up close.

As the chairman of the convention that year, I planned to do exactly that, but I admit I remember thinking, *Geez, I hope he's not mad at me.* Four years before, when I had been secretary of energy and Obama was running for Congress for the first time against the much more experienced Bobby Rush, I may have done something that upset Obama. Which is to say: I had picked Rush. I had backed the horse that ultimately beat him to the finish line. I had even attended a solar energy event on behalf of Rush and Chicago mayor Richard Daley. In short, I had dismissed Obama in favor of the establishment. I had no idea if Obama held a grudge, or had forgiven me.

Either way, as chairman of the convention he was about to address, I had a duty to reach out to him before his speech. I also wanted to suss out if I had an apology to make. So I called him.

"Is there anything I can do to help?"

His response was noncommittal.

"I understand you're chairman of the convention," he said. "I look forward to working with you."

I was afraid he was going to hit me head-on. *So what about that whole Bobby Rush thing?*

Because if I'm being honest, that's what I would have done.

Heck, that's what my wife, Barbara, would have done. She's always telling me, "Don't you remember when so-and-so said that thing about you? Are you really going to be nice to him now?" Holding a grudge is common among humans. It's practically mandatory for politicians (and the ones who remember the most: spouses).

Either Obama didn't recall, or he didn't think it productive to bring it up. Either way, it was a relief, and I appreciated either his poor memory or his generous restraint.

Thankfully, neither did he take me up on my offer to help. Truth is, although I had worked very hard to become 2004 chairman—even calling in a few favors, to be honest—I soon learned that it was a rather feckless position. Even though all the major candidates had to endorse me, and the position brought some visibility during ceremonial appearances at the convention, the only real power I had was to secure prime seating passes inside the auditorium for large Democratic supporters.

I was a high-profile, highly credentialed, highly visible Ticketmaster.

But you can be sure that I was determined to be one of the beneficiaries of my own superpower. Using the prerogative of the chairman, I assigned myself a front-row seat to see Barack Obama make his big debut. I wanted to see this guy in action, up close.

First, however, I was due to speak. I was a bit apprehensive, for a handful of reasons. First, I knew the most anticipated speech—that of the young Senate candidate from Chicago—would follow mine. (I counted my blessings that I wasn't due to follow his.) Second, I didn't want to come up short after comporting myself well during so many of the presidential debates over the past year. Finally, it was my second (and last) chance to make a first impression at the convention. I had been scheduled to give a speech on an earlier night—and I did—but Al Sharpton's speech just before mine had gone on so long my speech had been bumped past prime time. Even if I had summoned all my chairman powers of ticket distribution, it wouldn't have changed the fact that few people saw my performance that night. (Later, when as UN ambassador I hosted a party at the US Mission on behalf of Sharpton, I reminded him that he had bumped me. "Yeah, I remember," he chuckled. "That was a good speech of mine.")

My speech went well, but I could tell that the crowd in the auditorium was anticipating the next act; even they had heard the rumors. So right after I wrapped I headed backstage to meet the main event and introduce myself.

There Barack sat, apparently the opposite of nervous. He was composed, serene, and gracious, not only to me—his chairman, after all—but also to the tech crew and the stage manager as they brusquely walked him through the details of his presentation. Just moments before he was to be announced to the world, he got up and casually walked across the room to pour himself a cup of coffee. When he sat back down, he leaned back in his chair. No nervous tics. No need to fill the air with inane, anxious conversation. Composure personified.

Given a two-minute warning, he slowly and gracefully stood up. Michelle stepped toward him, picked some lint off his suit, and, as he turned to walk to the stage, said simply, "Knock 'em dead."

As history recalls, he did exactly that.

"As we speak, there are those who are preparing to divide us," he said, rousing an already receptive crowd.

"Well, I say to them tonight, there's not a liberal America and a conservative America; there's the United States of America."

Applause.

"There's not a black America and white America and Latino America and Asian America; there's the United States of America."

Growing cheers.

"The pundits, the pundits like to slice and dice our country into red states and blue states. . . . But I've got news for them, too. We worship an awesome God in the blue states, and we don't like federal agents poking around our libraries in the red states."

Massive applause.

"We coach Little League in the blue states and, yes, we've got some gay friends in the red states."

An entire auditorium, on its feet.

"There are patriots who opposed the war in Iraq, and there are patriots who supported the war in Iraq."

Rolling thunder.

"We are one people, all of us pledging allegiance to the Stars and Stripes, all of us defending the United States of America."

From my seat only sixty feet away, I had never seen anything like it. On almost every line, the cheers seemed to escalate. I had been to fifty conventions in my long political career, and never before had I experienced such a charged atmosphere built up by a simple speech, especially from a young, relatively unknown politician, a "skinny kid with a funny name." (By the way, for all the recitation and appreciation of his red/blue America line, that self-deprecating line about his appearance got as much applause as any other. It was my favorite.)

When he finally wrapped up, the fireworks continued. Or at least it looked like fireworks, as explosions of confetti fell down around all of us. Michelle stepped out from the wings and joined her husband on stage, looking just as comfortable and composed as she would four years later after becoming First Lady.

They took in the adulation for just a moment—not too long, wisely—and as they left the stage they walked right past me. They both waved together as they passed. With the deafening applause drowning out everything else, I could only mouth one word to them both: "Wow."

I quickly headed back to the holding area, where they were standing together. Still the applause was ringing. I said to him, "They're still cheering for you. Nice job."

He smiled and said, "Thank you."

Michelle smiled as well but didn't say anything. Instead, she just leaned in and hugged her husband. He may just have been a "skinny kid with a funny name," but now he was the undisputed heavyweight champion of the whole convention, and arguably of the entire Democratic Party.

With respect: Forget Kerry. Forget John Edwards. Their names may have been on the marquee—with hard-fought and well-earned victories in the Democratic primaries—but it was Obama that gave the star performance that night.

Thanks to a single speech—and a growing reputation as the future of the Democratic Party—Obama quickly became the most sought-after campaigner for other senators seeking either their first terms in Congress or reelection. They wanted him at every town hall and every fund-raiser. An impressive feat when you consider that *he hadn't even been elected yet himself.* He was a candidate helping other candidates—something you don't often see in the natural ecosystem of political races.

A few weeks after his bleacher-rattling speech at the convention, and surprising no one, Barack Obama won his own race for senator from Illinois, beating Alan Keyes with a whopping 70 percent of the vote. There may not have been a liberal America and a conservative America, but there certainly was an Obama Illinois.

I'll be honest. Even though I consider myself a political animal, I didn't see Obama coming. And yet, there he was, not only taking America by storm as an inspiring orator and a new senator, but also becoming a player on the international stage. Two years later, when I was summoned to Africa to help rescue *Chicago Tribune* reporter Paul Salopek from his detainment in Sudan, I learned that Obama had even beaten me to the punch halfway around the world; he had looked into Salopek's release while on a trip to Kenya.

It was also becoming clear that we might soon butt heads. I had intended to announce my candidacy for president in 2008. Even though conventional wisdom was that Obama wouldn't give it a go so early in his career, there were some tea leaves that suggested otherwise. It had all begun when Obama met with former senator Tom Daschle at Tosca, a restaurant in DC, and Tom urged him on: "Don't always think you will have another shot," he said. "You just never know what the future will hold." That kind of encouragement would appeal to anyone, let alone an ambitious, confident politico who had already achieved so much. A "skinny kid with a funny name" who reminded us that "in no other country on Earth is my story even possible."

Despite all the attention Obama was getting, I still thought if he ran for president, he'd be deemed too green. Clearly I was the naive one. But honestly, my concern as the 2008 presidential race approached wasn't the competition I might have with

Obama. My concern was Hillary Clinton. And frankly, Hillary's concern was John Edwards. Edwards's concern, it would turn out, was his own demons. And even after Obama did ultimately announce, he debuted twenty points behind Hillary. It seemed he had jumped the gun.

I saw Obama again at the annual meeting of the Democratic National Committee in DC. Hard to believe that the last time I'd seen him he had been making his debut and running for national office for the first time. Now we were both candidates for the presidency of the United States of America. What a difference four years makes.

Still, as much as Obama-the-phenomenon had been launched, Obama-the-candidate hadn't yet caught on. He was polling rather low and needed to make a few more impressive impressions to become a contender. The DNC meeting was such an opportunity. It is a cattle show, when all the candidates get a chance to address the delegates who will return to the all-important (if all-presaged) Democratic convention. By some accounts, I gave the best speech that day. And when I retired to the room I had been assigned to greet supporters, I was mobbed. I couldn't help but think: *I may have a chance at this thing.* And just a little bit: *Barack who?* It was a heady night.

As they always are in presidential election years, the debates were a blur. But again, I had the good fortune to be placed next to Obama in many debates, and I got to know him in the strangest of circumstances, as we were able to gossip a bit while on stage. People are often surprised to hear how much candidates have the opportunity to chat even while the cameras are rolling. "Are you going to that Lance Armstrong thing?" "Did you see that hatchet job in the *Times*?" "Where are you headed after this?"

Obama and I would also hang out in the greenroom before

and after each debate. As I often do, I played around with the pronunciation of his name. In his case, I'd over-enunciate the syllables. "O-Ba-Ma!" I'd say. He seemed to get a kick out of it. Ultimately he shot back, "Get to know that name, Rich-Ard-Son," he said. "I'm gonna be around." It wasn't arrogance; it was confidence. And it was convincing.

He wasn't gracious just to his fellow candidates—I remind you, had he not rescued me on the Katrina question, I would have faltered early on—but to everyone. Janitors, security guards, caterers, local police—he had time to talk to anyone and everyone who approached him. I noticed that he never read from the typical politician script—"I'm Barack Obama, and I'm asking for your vote." He made no such plea; he just wanted to say hello. And early on, he didn't have much of an entourage, so he seemed accessible to all. And to all, he'd offer a vigorous handshake.

As someone who holds a handshaking record, even I was impressed.

I don't want to imply that I was his best pal, or that I had a special relationship with him. Our conversations were cordial and friendly, but we weren't exactly divulging our deepest secrets and wildest dreams to each other. But I was getting to know Obama the person as well as Obama the candidate, and the more time I spent with him, the more I enjoyed his company.

To say the least, I wasn't alone. Despite the slow start, the Obama bandwagon began to build up a thick head of steam, and adoring crowds started to show up in droves. Twentysomethings. Fortysomethings. Eightysomethings. His growing mass appeal started to intimidate other candidates. After he sold out two appearances in the early primary state of New Hampshire, Indiana senator Evan Bayh dropped out of the race, suggesting that "the odds were longer than I felt I could responsibly pursue."

Honestly, the odds were getting longer for all of us. For my part, I was irritated early on that the whole enterprise was being characterized as a Hillary/Edwards/Obama race. Edwards, because he had run before and was keeping up a solid showing in Iowa. Hillary because she was Hillary. Obama because of the momentum that had grown, slowly but surely, since his introductory speech in Boston in 2004. In most debates I was being treated as a distant fourth because, well, because I *was* a distant fourth.

But I still felt I was performing well, and immodestly I say I wasn't alone in feeling that way. Even the conservative columnist David Brooks put out his neck to support me. In his *New York Times* op-ed assertively titled "Neither Clinton, Nor Obama," he called me "recognizably human, unlike some of his overpolished peers." And although he found me "baggy-faced, sloppy . . . and inelegant," I was also "garrulous [and] amusing." On substance, however, I had an edge: "He is, after all, the most experienced person running for president." And "when it comes to policy positions," he pointed out, "he's perfectly positioned—not by accident—to carry liberals and independents." All told, "It becomes absurdly easy to picture him rising toward the top. . . . He's the candidate most likely to rise."

I didn't rise. At least not enough. And although I was willing to see my increasingly quixotic campaign through a bit longer—I was enjoying myself, and campaigns have a way of surprising you, so I continued to think anything could happen—I had to begin contemplating whom I might support if I were to withdraw.

I was well aware that most observers expected I would, out of pure loyalty to Bill Clinton, be obligated to endorse his wife.

I didn't buy that logic. For one simple reason: Bill wasn't on the ticket. His wife hadn't appointed me energy secretary or UN ambassador. For all I knew, she may even have lobbied against me for the positions.

At the Iowa state convention, where each candidate was given ten minutes to try to rouse their supporters in a packed but small basketball stadium, I ran into Chicago native Bill Daley. Like me, Bill had worked for President Clinton in the '90s. You may recall that Bill famously had fainted in the White House pressroom when he and I were appointed to the president's team on the same day. So we were in a similar boat: We had both navigated the occasionally rough waters of the Clinton administration.

Despite that history—despite an assumed obligation to be loyal to the captain of the ship—Bill Daley had already announced his support of Obama for president. I couldn't let the moment pass, because there was something I had to know. "Bill, I know you're supporting Obama," I said. "I gotta ask: Are the Clintons pissed at you?" It was clear that Bill had thought about it before—that incurring the famed Clinton wrath was a distinct possibility—but Bill smiled, because he had found a great excuse to throw his weight behind Obama. "Hey, I'm from Chicago. He's my senator." He had political cover to follow his heart. But I had to give him a hard time. "Yeah, he's been your senator. For about three days!" He laughed. He knew I was calling him out on his convenient justification. I had to assume he wondered if it would actually fly with the Clintons.

I certainly did.

I knew that my decision would come down to two candidates: Hillary Clinton or Barack Obama. And that the entire process would be one long negotiation (with myself as much as with the candidates). Obama's ten-minute speech in Iowa didn't make my decision any easier. He was spectacular. He talked of big themes: Unity and Bipartisanship and The Future. I turned to my wife and said something that shocked her: "Barbara, I'm seriously thinking of tossing my speech aside and just going up there and endorsing him right now. Forget the speech. It's irrelevant now. I should just endorse him!" She shot me a look: *Are you crazy?*

She didn't have to say a word. She was right. It was too soon.

We continued campaigning, and although I still felt it might prove to be a losing battle—so often I was told by voters that it came down to me or Obama, and they were choosing Obama—I found those many months to be a thoroughly enriching experience. I would even say that the smaller crowds I drew were a pleasant silver lining. I could shake almost everyone's hand, whereas Obama's crowds were just too immense to give that up-close-and-personal, tactile satisfaction. Eventually, Obama was even assigned a Secret Service detail, further distancing him from the voters he hoped to greet. (I don't fool myself into thinking it cost him votes; it just cost him the delight of meeting his supporters individually.)

At the Iowa steak fry, sponsored by the Hawkeye State's senator Tom Harkin in Indianola—a traditional event to "meat and greet" the all-important early-voting citizens of the state—I gave another strong speech, this time in a big green pasture filled with corn-fed patriots. I don't doubt that the devil-may-care, nothing-to-lose attitude that characterized my campaign freed me to speak dynamically and colorfully. The reviews across the board were positive. "Good speech," Obama said, as I returned to my seat.

The stakes were higher for Obama, but it wasn't what he said or didn't say that drew the most attention that day. It's what he didn't *do*. As the national anthem poured from the loudspeakers, the candidates stepped forward and turned slightly to the right to face the flag. Barack stood closest to it, with me, Hillary, and Tom Harkin's wife, Ruth, in line behind him. Everyone put their hands over their hearts—everyone, that is, except Barack.

I tell you now there was nothing malicious or unpatriotic about Obama's choice, nor did he have the benefit of seeing that everyone behind him had fallen in line. It was an innocent mistake. We've all had our moments of absentmindedness at the most inopportune times on the campaign trail; this was his turn.

Yet considering the persistent rumors among the right-wing crowd—that Obama is a Kenyan-born Muslim socialist who was sworn in on a Koran and refuses to recite the Pledge of Allegiance—I suppose it wasn't surprising that the press would jump all over the trumped-up controversy, trumping it up even further. I received a handful of e-mails saying various versions of "Thank you for putting your hand over your heart." No thanks were necessary; frankly, and I say this as a patriot, I don't remember thinking it was that big of a deal at the time.

And—hand to my heart—I still don't.

But the anti-American drumbeat continued. Obama was also being criticized for his choice not to wear a flag pin on his lapel when he didn't feel it was appropriate ("Sometimes I wear it, sometimes I don't") and never when he felt it was a weak substitute for real patriotism ("My attitude is that I'm less concerned about what you're wearing on your lapel than what's in your heart"). Nonetheless, he ultimately relented, and he began to wear the pin far more often than I suspect he'd planned to. I understand why; sometimes it's easier to go along than to go alone.

Throughout this assault, he appeared from where I was standing—once again, right next to him—to be unflappable. Dignified. Dare I say it, *presidential.*

I knew that the closer I got to withdrawing and throwing my support behind another candidate, the tougher the decision would be: Did I owe it to the Clintons to support Hillary, or did I owe it to myself to support whomever I wished?

The Iowa caucuses forced the issue. They also were the first test of just how angry the Clintons might get if I were to endorse Anyone But Hillary. John Harwood, the chief Washington correspondent for CNBC and a columnist for the *New York Times*, went live with a report in the *Times* declaring that if I didn't receive enough votes to cross the threshold in Iowa, I had agreed to send my delegates over to the Obama camp.

No doubt the Clintons thought it was traitorous, treasonous, and disloyal.

I thought it was bullshit.

I had made no such deal.

To say that I was angry is only half of it. I knew that when Hillary and Bill caught wind of the reckless lie, they'd bring the hammer down on me. They weren't the only ones. I received call after call inquiring whether the rumors were true, and I got hoarse from all the times I had to deny them. Friends of the campaign called. Reporters called. Lanny Davis, who had served as special counsel to President Clinton, called and said he had heard from a trusted source that I had made the deal. I kept insisting it wasn't true.

Wasn't it?

I certainly didn't remember striking any deal. But when Obama's campaign manager, David Plouffe, having been asked if the story was true, didn't deny it outright—he said only that "no formal arrangements" had been made—I began to reconsider my own sanity. *Had* I made the arrangement? Or, rather, had someone made the arrangement on my behalf?

I grilled all my top aides. They all pleaded either innocence or ignorance.

Only days later, after Obama famously won Iowa in a surprise upset—and I came in, as usual, a rousing fourth—did I learn that the rumors had been true all along. One of my staffers in Iowa *had* made such a deal, and only because I've since forgiven him do I choose not to mention his name here.

My fourth-place finish bought me—just barely—a spot in the next debate in New Hampshire. And as we took the stage in Manchester, just before the cameras were about to roll, Obama leaned in to my ear and said, "Hey, man, thanks for Iowa." It took everything I had not to lean back into his ear and say, "I had no fucking idea." Instead I said nothing. All I knew is that if Obama thought I had sent him votes, you could be damn sure that the Clintons—who by this point were looking for indications of what I was thinking—would be sure of it. They'd be fuming, and although I had been naive to it, they had at least one reason to be angry. But the absurdity wasn't lost on me: They'd be pissed at me for doing something even I didn't know I had done.

In the debate that began just minutes later, by every indication but the one that mattered—my sagging poll numbers—I performed quite well. The pollster Frank Luntz, who often held town halls immediately following these debates, even reported that among those who actually watched the darn thing, I came out ahead of Obama. But my overall numbers were still low, and I remained in last place. When New Hampshire went to the polls, I received just 5 percent of the vote.

It was time to withdraw.

After consulting with my advisors in New Mexico, I held a final rally in my beloved hometown of Santa Fe.

"It is with great pride, understanding, and acceptance that I am ending my campaign for president of the United States," I said. "The time has come to end my quest and come home to tackle the challenges before us in New Mexico."

The crowd cheered, and many took to their feet. Of course, I couldn't miss the opportunity to joke around.

"I'm noticing who's not standing up," I said.

As for the rest of the field of presidential candidates of which I would no longer be a part, I took the opportunity to praise each of them remaining, because as I said in my speech, we should "disagree on policy, but respect the . . . personal integrity of the others running." If I'm being honest, I also thought I needed to tamp down the heat I was feeling from the Clinton campaign, and that an honest and evenhanded compliment might help.

"Senator Edwards is a singular voice for the most downtrodden and forgotten among us," I said, not knowing that he'd soon be largely forgotten himself.

"Senator Obama is a bright light of hope and optimism at a time of great national unease, yet he is also grounded in thoughtful wisdom beyond his years," I said, not knowing that he'd ultimately need every ounce of that wisdom to run the country.

"Senator Clinton's poise in the face of adversity is matched only by her lifetime of achievement and deep understanding of the challenges we face," I said, not knowing if my words would fall on deaf ears.

I thanked my supporters, I thanked my staff, and I said goodbye to my dream of being the president of the United States.

It was the right decision, although I admit I was just a little hurt that so many reports of my withdrawal contained some version of the phrase *as widely anticipated*. I mean, c'mon! I may be a politician and have thick skin, but that stung a bit!

But the reports were right:

On Thursday, January 10, 2008, my quest for the presidency ended.

And the real negotiation began.

The calls came fast and furious, with each candidate hoping to persuade me to endorse their candidacy as soon as possible. The first call, unsurprisingly, came from Hillary. The next from Obama. Then Edwards. For a few days, it seemed they were each running two campaigns: one for the presidency, and one for my endorsement.

Each waged their assault on my cell phone with a different and inimitable style unique to them. The most striking difference in approach was between Obama and Clinton. Obama's calls were consistent, about one per week. "Hey, man, it's O-Ba-Ma," he'd say, continuing the game we'd played on the campaign trail. They weren't pleading calls; they were thoughtful, soft, gentle persuasion. I never doubted he was trying to negotiate an endorsement out of me, but I never felt like he was desperate for it.

What's more, Barack's calls were personal, always from his cell phone direct to mine. He put on no airs. There was no "Please hold for Senator Obama." It was his voice in my ear, just as it had been his voice in my ear months earlier, rescuing me from embarrassment when I hadn't heard the question about Katrina in the debate. One to one. Considerate. Careful. Cool.

Whereas Hillary's calls always began the same way: "Please hold for Senator Clinton." Often her calls would come from her fund-raisers. Elizabeth Bagley called. Haim Saban. Mickey Kantor. It wasn't exactly the personal touch.

When Hillary called, I would often have to wait until her assistant announced that she would soon come on the line. Now, let the record show I'm a patient man, but at the time I was also the governor of New Mexico. There was no reason to keep me waiting, either.

From a negotiation standpoint, she was misfiring. She was "playing status," subtly implying her time was more valuable than mine. In a negotiation, when you want something from someone else, it's never a good idea to start each negotiation session with them resenting you, even on the smallest matters.

Edwards stopped calling, and for a good reason. A few weeks after I dropped out, so too did he. In a speech in the Ninth Ward of New Orleans, he said he was leaving the race "so history can blaze its path." As we now know, there may have been other reasons, too.

So then there were two. The calls from Hillary and Barack kept coming, and kept reinforcing their respective styles. Hillary's calls were pleading, insistent, direct. Barack's remained cool, calm, almost passive. But he was laying the groundwork for the question, not asking it directly. The most transparent he ever got was a calculated attempt to tug on my heartstrings. "Hey, man," he said. "We can make history. Let's make some history together. You, me, and Teddy." Ted Kennedy had chosen to support Obama. Invoking his name might have been a clever ploy, but from a man who was making history himself—as the first African American with a real shot at the White House—it seemed sincere.

Throughout the entire process, Barack's soft touch never wavered. It reminded me of the time we were both campaigning in Las Cruces, New Mexico, at a veterans' memorial. As we stood there paying our respects, a gust of wind knocked down the symbolic wreath that stood on an easel in front of a tombstone. Without missing a beat, Obama picked the wreath up and replaced it, as anyone—and certainly any politician—might have done. But Obama went a step further, painstakingly picking up each fallen flower and returning it to its rightful place.

He wasn't doing it for the cameras. He was doing it for the soldiers.

A soft touch. An effective touch.

His calls to me were never transactional, and these things can be. He never said, "What do you want if I win?" He just said, as a simple matter of fact, "I'm going to win, Bill. Mathematically, I'm going to win." For her part, even as her path to victory slipped away, Hillary denied the facts, and the math. "There's no way he can win," she'd tell me.

There were a few good reasons both candidates wanted to pin down my support in particular. On a practical level, I had many Hispanic supporters I could send their way. What's more, the columnist Bill Kristol and others implied that whoever received my endorsement could very well win Texas's fast-approaching March primary, and thereby win the presidency. That might be exaggerating things a bit, but the remaining candidates were approaching panic mode. Had I still been in the race, I would have felt the same way.

So I owed it to both candidates to either put up or shut up. To endorse or not to endorse.

It's true there were more than enough criteria to make an informed decision. They might both be Democrats, and they might have seen eye-to-eye on the lion's share of the policy issues, but there was still enough contrast to go on. Hillary had spent almost two decades in the national spotlight;

Obama had spent three years. Hillary was old school; Obama was new blood.

On one important issue, I couldn't help but lean toward Obama. My instinct was that while Obama would bring a new, excited throng of people into DC, Hillary would surround herself with the same old Washington insiders that I had known throughout my time in the Clinton administration. It seemed time to turn the page. (I recognize the irony, that as a longtime Clinton appointee, I was arguing against people just like me.)

Obama also shared my foreign policy view that it's acceptable—heck, it's often preferable—to talk to foreign leaders whom we disagree with "without precondition." At one debate in late February, when asked if he would meet with leaders in Cuba—something I know a little bit about—Obama said, "Not just in Cuba, but I think this principle applies generally." He even cited John F. Kennedy: "We should never negotiate out of fear, but we should never fear to negotiate." On this point Hillary Clinton disagreed, insisting that meeting without preconditions "undermines the capacity for us to actually take the measure of someone like Raúl Castro."

How so? I still don't understand that logic. How better to take the measure of someone like Raúl Castro than to meet Raúl Castro? I can guarantee you there's a much more fruitful negotiation to be had after the negotiators have chosen to negotiate. Makes sense, doesn't it?

Still, while the distinctions were clear, the choice was not. And the fact that Bill Clinton invited himself over to watch the Super Bowl with me didn't exactly make the decision any easier. I knew he'd lean on me hard. I knew he could be very convincing. I wondered if I'd buckle under his powers of persuasion. And when Obama heard that Clinton was jetting my way, he called.

"I can't compete with that," he said.

"Compete with what?" I asked, although I knew what he was aiming at.

"I can't compete with an ex-president coming to see you."

"I understand," I said. "But I'm not ready to endorse. So I'll make a promise to you. I won't make a decision while he's here. That's all I can do right now."

"I'll take it," he said. "But Bill, are you sure that's a promise you can keep?" he asked, laughing. "Bill Clinton is a very persuasive man."

"Tell you what," I said. "I'll do my best."

Clinton arrived, and although it was one of the more awkward few hours of my life, I managed to get through all four quarters of the Super Bowl without pledging to him my firstborn—or my endorsement. He was upset, but I was relieved. I had kept my promise.

Not the next day, not the day after that, but a few days later, I received a call I had been expecting much earlier.

"Bill, it's O-Ba-Ma."

Of course it is.

"I noticed you haven't endorsed," he said.

"That's right," I said.

"So I still have a shot."

"You do," I said.

"So we can keep talking?" he asked.

"We can, yes."

"That's all I ask," he said.

He didn't ask for my endorsement right then and there, even though it must have been tempting. But he knew he was in the middle of the negotiation, not the end stage, and pressing his case might backfire. It's always important to gauge where your negotiating partner is in his thought process, and on this occasion Obama deciphered it masterfully; he could tell that I wasn't ready to commit.

The truth is, I didn't know what I planned to do. My staff was leaning toward Obama (many of them had joined the Obama campaign after I dropped out), and they were twisting my arm to follow suit. For them, the choice was clear.

But only I knew the true tangle of the complications involved. My relationship with the Clintons was—and remains—complex. I had worked closely with Bill for the better part of a decade, and it's an indisputable fact that he paved a path for me to thrive in not one but two high-profile national positions: secretary of energy and US ambassador to the United Nations. But it's also a fact—I humbly suggest—that I deserved those opportunities.

So it's wrong to say I owed them nothing. And it's not fair to say I owed them everything.

It was my decision to make.

But that didn't mean I couldn't use a little help. After losing some sleep over the decision, I decided to reach out to two trusted advisors—good friends over many decades—to get second and third opinions, since I was having trouble forming a first opinion. I asked them two questions that I needed to answer: one, if I were to endorse Obama over Hillary, was that truly being disloyal to Bill Clinton? And two, if it was disloyal, did I owe Clinton so much that I shouldn't endorse Obama anyhow?

The first response I received was direct.

Bill, my advisor said, *you have to remember that the Clintons are politicians. Heck, they're the most political couple we've ever met. And that means they're all about themselves. This isn't a criticism, it's a fact. If you're useful to them, they'll continue courting you. If you're not useful to them, they'll forget about you. They may not forgive, but they'll forget. They'll move on. And it's true that Bill helped you over the years, but hey, let's remember you did a lot for him as well. You helped him navigate the Lewinsky mess. You were always there for him when he needed to talk, complain, vent, on all those late-night phone calls. You were there during the tough times. If you ask me, your debt is repaid. So you have to realize you have the flexibility to do what you want, to do what's right for you. So if you want to go with Obama— and we can be honest, it's a calculating political move, and I think you recognize that—but if you really want to go with Obama, you should go with your heart. You have that freedom.*

I perhaps wouldn't have gone so far to say that my debt had been repaid—and certainly not that Clinton owed me— but the second call helped put what debt I still had left in even sharper context.

You've had a good career doing what Bill Richardson does best: be Bill Richardson. Bill Clinton didn't make you. Sure, he helped you, but he didn't make you. He appointed you to two important positions—true—but you put yourself in the position to be appointed, and when you got there, you did the work. Not him. What you've accomplished is not because of Bill Clinton. It's because of Bill Richardson.

Honestly, the calls felt a little like therapy sessions, but that doesn't mean what was said wasn't true. And they were certainly helpful. After another night's sleep—this one less fitful—I was ready to make my decision. Actually, my decision had been made.

I waited for the next time Senator Obama called.

"Bill! It's O-Ba-Ma!" he began, as he always did. "How you doin'?"

A little small talk never hurts.

"Me? I'm good, I'm good. You?"

"I'm good."

There was an elephant in the room, but instead we talked about how two donkeys were feeling.

"Yeah, I'm good," I said. "How's the campaign trail?"

"It's good. How's it being back in Santa Fe?"

"It's good."

Everything was good.

The ball was in my court—it was my obligation, not his, to turn the conversation to the endorsement—but I didn't say anything right away. Perhaps I enjoyed the power of keeping him on the hook and on the line. Or maybe I was giving him one last chance to say something crazy that changed my mind.

Finally I gave him what he wanted.

"O-Ba-Ma," I said. "I've made a decision."

He said nothing. He wisely wanted to let me unspool the details on my terms. So I continued:

"And it's gonna be you."

And that's when the man known worldwide as one of history's greatest orators said . . . nothing. He may not have been speechless—that's presuming too much on my part—but he certainly was silent. My impression: He was shocked.

"I'm endorsing you," I said, just to make sure the message was clear.

More silence.

Finally, in a whisper we've rarely heard from the president—and I recalled only from my Katrina moment—he said, "Man, I really appreciate it."

Then more silence.

I let it hang there, just in case he wanted to expound on his gratitude. (Hey, can you blame me? It was no small thing I was doing for him.) But he said nothing more. I considered the possibility that the line had gone dead.

I took the reins back. "There's just one problem," I said. "A logistical issue."

He appeared to still be collecting himself, so I went on: "I promised my wife, Barbara, that I'd take her to the Caribbean." Many months earlier, Barbara and I had planned to get away from it all—and recover from the draining campaign—by heading to Mill Reef in Antigua. "So," I said, resolutely, "we're going to the Caribbean."

"How is that a problem?" Obama said, laughing.

Aha, he's still with me.

"I'm ready to endorse you, but we're leaving soon and we're not gonna be back for another week or so," I explained.

"I hear you," Obama said.

He didn't seem to be catching on. I thought the problem was implied, frankly; Senator Obama was in the throes of dealing with the revelation that his longtime pastor, Reverend Jeremiah Wright, had been caught on tape preaching wildly anti-American sermons. The campaigns were frantically courting superdelegates they could count on should the election turn out to be razor thin, and the Wright fiasco had to be unnerving a few Obama supporters. Surely he would want to use my endorsement as a way to change the subject. That was on my mind, so it must have been on his.

"So how should we handle the endorsement?" I asked. "An announcement? Should I record something today you can play while I'm away?"

"No, no, no," he said. He'd clearly thought this through. "We've got to do it together. Just you and me, onstage. At a rally."

"But my wife would kill me if I canceled our—"

"No, don't cancel. I'm not asking you to cancel. Take your vacation, by all means," he said.

For a man rushing toward history, he seemed to be in no hurry. A cool customer, even during the heat of the Wright scandal.

"And when you come back," he said, "we'll do a major event. It'll be fun."

He said he'd consult with his staff to determine the best time and place for the announcement. And with that, Barbara and I headed to the white-sand beaches of Antigua for some much-needed rest and relaxation.

Despite the idyllic locale, I can't say our vacation was free of anxiety. Both Barbara and I knew that my endorsement of Obama, while invigorating for me personally, was bound to bring some headaches. Between sips of more than a few umbrella drinks, we couldn't help but talk about the decision. And more important, what that decision meant.

"I love you," Barbara said, "and I'm with you. And I support you. But you know what you have to do."

It's true. I knew exactly what she was referring to. She didn't have to explain further. Sometime between the relaxation of Antigua and the thrill of the endorsement, I had to do something that wasn't thrilling and certainly wasn't relaxing.

I had to call the Clintons.

When we got back to Santa Fe, I called Obama. "O-Ba-Ma!" I said. "It's Rich-Ard-Son."

He was glad to hear from me, and even gladder to hear that I hadn't gotten cold feet. On the contrary, the more I had thought about my decision, the more sure I had been that it was the right one. That turned out to be the easy part.

"So how do you want to do this?" I asked.

He explained that after consulting with his staff, he had determined that I should join him in Portland, Oregon, on March 21. He would charter a jet, fly me and some members of my staff up to the Beaver State, and we'd throw a rally. Sounded good to me. I'm always up for a rally.

The night before the trip, I picked up the phone again. I took a breath, stiffened my spine, and dialed Hillary. Just to amuse myself—I tend to get silly when I'm nervous—I had the briefest inclination to say this when she answered: "Please hold for the governor."

I did not.

I'm fairly certain she wouldn't have gotten the joke.

Instead, I calmly told her my plans to endorse Obama the next day.

Unlike Obama, she was not shocked to hear the news. But she was upset.

"Don't do it, Bill. That's a huge mistake."

I asked her what she meant specifically.

"Because he can't win. He won't win," she said, as matter-of-fact as she could. As if it were a simple truth of the universe.

As a politician, I know the inclination to write off your fellow candidates as nonstarters, specifically the ones causing you the most trouble. But if Barack truly had had no chance, Hillary wouldn't have had to be so insistent about it. It's not that she was protesting too much, it was that she was protesting at all.

"He won't win, and you'll be the guy who backed the wrong candidate," she said. "Bill, I'm telling you, *don't.*"

She continued to plead with me, even after it was evident she wouldn't change my mind. Though I don't think she considered it wasted breath. I suspect she felt she did a decent job of planting doubts about my choice in my mind, even if she hadn't changed it. At the very least, she might be able to tell me *I told you so.*

That's always an impulse in a negotiation: Even when you don't get what you want, it's tempting to get if not *the* last word, then a few last words that make your fellow negotiator at least doubt whether he or she has made the right decision. It's tempting, but it's a mistake. Nobody likes being told *I told you so*, and being told *I told you so* doesn't make anybody like the person who said *I told you so* better just because they told you so. (That makes sense, so read it again if you're confused. See? Told you so.)

And if anybody asks who told you so, you can tell 'em Bill Richardson told you so.

Anyhow, at some point Hillary gave up. And I thought I had gotten through the worst of it, but then she asked, "Are you going to call the president?" Meaning Bill, not Bush. Frankly, I had hoped that this one call would suffice for the pair of them (after all, don't they come as a team? Isn't that why I was expected to be loyal to Hillary? Wasn't that the bargain?). Now she was putting yet another uncomfortable call on my agenda. So I said, "Absolutely."

We hung up.

I made a few more calls, perhaps as warmups to the main event. I phoned Madeleine Albright, who had served as Bill Clinton's secretary of state when I was UN ambassador and energy secretary. I told her my decision, and she too was disappointed, and although she didn't go as far as to say I was making a huge mistake, she did do a decent job of taking some wind out of my sails. I called Henry Cisneros, who had been Clinton's secretary of housing and urban development. Henry and I had been friends for decades, but even he expressed some misgivings about my choice.

My warmups weren't exactly warming me up.

Still, I knew I couldn't delay any longer. My flight to Portland was leaving in a matter of hours.

I summoned some courage and called Bill.

Ring.

Ring.

Ring.

It beeped through to voicemail.

I wouldn't get to talk to him directly. I might have been relieved, but I wasn't. There was too much to address.

I needed to tell him all the things I should have told him during the Super Bowl. I needed to tell him that despite his help in my career during the '90s, I had to make certain decisions in 2008. I needed to tell him that although I was one of the old Clinton hands myself, I truly believed the country needed a new vision from a new generation of public servants. I needed to tell him that although I was loyal to him, it wasn't clear to me why that loyalty was also owed to his wife. And I needed to tell him that even though I would have rather spoken with him in person, I had had to leave all this on his voicemail because tomorrow morning I would be boarding a plane to Oregon to endorse Senator Obama.

Instead I said, "Bill, it's Bill. Call me back when you can."

He never called me back.

The next morning at 6:00 a.m., I boarded the plane to Oregon, knowing that the die had already been cast. The rally wasn't until 10:00 a.m. Pacific, but Obama and I had agreed that the

Associated Press would be sent a statement at 3:00 a.m. I didn't look at the headlines before we taxied down the runway and took off. Not because I wasn't interested. I just imagined Bill Clinton reading over my shoulder to learn from the AP what I should have told him last night. One man's good day is another man's bad news.

After we landed in Portland and drove to the Memorial Coliseum, where the rally would be held, I must say that any thoughts of Bill (and, further, Hillary and Edwards and Joe Biden and Christopher Dodd and Dennis Kucinich and Mike Gravel) simply vanished. The air was electric, and it was all for Obama. Thousands had shown up, and when I got to the greenroom to meet the man of the hour, I was told they had estimated that thirteen thousand had already crowded into the stadium to see him. (I was told the Beatles had played there once, and they had managed twenty thousand. And there were *four* of them. I'd say we measured up nicely.)

You could feel the buzz—and the chants of "Yes We Can"—permeating into our holding area, and when Obama greeted me, even he had a look on his face that said, *Can you believe this?*

"All these people, here to see me!" I joked.

He laughed, but when the moment came, even the announcer seemed to get it wrong. "Ladies and gentlemen," he said, "please welcome Governor Bill Richardson!"

I got first billing, and I must say, the cheers were nice.

"And Senator Barack Obama!"

But these cheers? These cheers were deafening.

When we took the stage—together, as he had suggested—there was a huge ovation. And it was then that I saw the country, for a moment, as Barack Obama must have seen it. A sea of young, eager Americans hopeful for a change. Minorities.

Teenagers. Types of people I had never seen at rallies before. Their intensity wasn't just palpable. You could have powered the stadium lights off their charge.

Even when Obama motioned for me to take the podium, the cheers continued. "O-Ba-Ma! O-Ba-Ma!" I waited for a whole two minutes before I could begin, but then I said what I had come for:

"Earlier this week," I began, "an extraordinary American gave a historic speech." The cheers rose again. They knew what I was referring to. Just days before, Obama had given what's now called his *race speech* to address the Jeremiah Wright controversy, and most observers count it among his most compelling. Many believe it saved his candidacy.

"He could have given a safer speech," I said. "He could have waited for the controversy over the deplorable remarks of Reverend Wright to subside. . . . Instead, Senator Obama showed us once again what kind of leader he is."

What kind of leader is he? Even though we were in Oregon, I was happy to invoke the sentiment of another historic politician from Illinois.

"Senator Obama has started a discussion in this country [that is] long overdue and rejects the politics of pitting race against race. . . . His words are those of a courageous, thoughtful, and inspiring leader who understands that a house divided against itself cannot stand."

I had made my decision a week earlier, but it's true that Obama's speech had clinched it for me. I had made the right decision.

I went on to praise Obama's vision in opposing the Iraq War from the beginning—he knew back then what others learned only much later; in championing an issue dear to my heart, renewable energy; and in his obvious innate skills as a politician:

"As we campaigned against each other for the presidency, I came to fully appreciate his steadfast patriotism and remarkable talents."

But as I looked out at all the adoring young people, I knew they already agreed with me. They were cheering, after all. So right here I went off script, because I had one more story to tell. One they hadn't heard.

"And I also realized that here was a really good guy. And I'll tell you why. I'll tell you why. I'll tell you why. You all watched those long, tedious Democratic debates, right?"

If you watch the video of the endorsement, this is the point where Obama can clearly tell where I'm heading. He looks at the floor with a sheepish grin.

"I could barely get recognized in any of 'em! But one time when I *was* recognized, and I was sitting next to Senator Obama, and I said, 'Finally I've been recognized.' So I turned to him and we started chatting a little bit. Then all of a sudden, the moderator—instead of going after other candidates that hadn't been recognized—came back to me, and asked me to answer the question! Well, needless to say, I wasn't listening!"

I laughed as I said it, which amplified tenfold the laughter coming back at me.

"So I turned to Senator Obama in horror, about to say to the moderator, 'Could you repeat the question?' That's when Senator Obama whispered to me.

"He leaned in and he said, '*Katrina.*'"

President Barack Obama has inspired many. He has disappointed some. As the chief executive of the United States, responsible for the welfare of the most powerful country on Earth, that's about as good a ratio as one can expect.

It's a tough job.

You try to "preserve, protect, and defend" the Constitution while commanding the world's strongest army. It ain't so easy.

I am not going to render judgment on his time in office as he still has a full term to go. I have, however, supported many of his policies and forcefully defended him many times on TV. I also campaigned for him in 2012. I can and will suggest that he negotiated his path *to* the office masterfully, despite all those who doubted him.

It was too soon, they said. He disagreed, and he proved them wrong.

He was too green, they said, until he charmed both blue and red America.

The country is not ready for an African American president, they said, and not even Obama can change that. Well, ready or not, here he comes.

And Yes He Can.

As a candidate, Senator Obama navigated all the potential pitfalls of a bruising presidential campaign—and there were many, from Reverend Jeremiah Wright to the Weather Underground to "you're likable enough, Hillary"—with not only the aplomb of a confident man but also the vision of a chess master.

I was there; I saw it firsthand.

And when I glimpsed his generosity up close—as I had when he rescued me during that presidential debate—I was literally only feet away. He was so near he could have reached out and pushed me down. Instead he extended his hand and pulled me from the quicksand.

It had been the perfect start to a negotiation. At that

moment, he had earned my trust. I had learned right then his principle of negotiation: Be competitive, but not cruel.

Truth is, I keep coming back to that Katrina moment. As I told that adoring crowd in Oregon, "He could have thrown me under the bus"—most politicians would have. But instead, "he stood behind me." The stadium shook with applause and appreciation. Many of the accounts of my endorsement that day made special mention of that moment. I understand why. That kind of grace is rare to find anywhere, and it's practically extinct in politics.

Throughout the entire campaign for my endorsement, Obama had gotten it right. He hadn't negotiated with me as much as he had given me the time and space to negotiate with myself, to come to the conclusion in my head that I had already reached in my heart. Instead of the hard sell, he had offered the soft touch. He had not pleaded. He had led.

And I had followed.

Billy the Kid:

AT THE END OF ANY term in office, there's always some tidying up to do. Desks cleaned out. Budgets settled. Computers sabotaged just to mess with the next guy. (If anyone asks, I'm kidding about that last one.)

But for executives—which is to say, presidents and governors—there's a unique end-zone responsibility that comes with the gig. As the clock on a term ticks down to zero, as stated in the United States Constitution's Article II, Section 2, presidents "shall have the power to grant reprieves and pardons for offenses against the United States." They have the power, and they have used it. George Washington himself got things rolling in 1795, when he granted the first presidential pardons to Philip Vigol and John Mitchell, who had been convicted of treason—and sentenced to hang—for protesting against the tax on liquor during the Whiskey Rebellion. Washington was a trendsetter; as history unfolded and this young country called America accumulated its share of criminals, pardons became more and more popular. There were more than twenty thousand presidential pardons in the twentieth century alone.

States can get in the game too. In the more than forty states that don't have a specially designated parole board, governors like me also have the authority to offer clemency or reprieve to those who have committed offenses against the State. These are often matters of life and death. Illinois governor George Ryan and my predecessor, New Mexico governor Toney Anaya, both offered blanket commutations to everyone on death row.

Pardons, it's fair to say, are almost always controversial. There's usually a good reason criminals were sent to prison in the first place—often it's something about *having committed a crime*—and there are at least a few people who want that person to stay guilty. Often, pardons are subject to accusations of favor repayment or partisanship. The underlying idea—that freely given grace makes us humans all the more humane—is honorable.

But it's touchy.

As he left office after pardoning financier and tax dodger Marc Rich—who, according to then–US prosecutor Rudy Giuliani, committed "the biggest tax evasion case in United States history"—President Clinton practically had to wear a coat of armor for all the flak he was getting. He must have known it would come his way. Rich's wife, Denise, had made large contributions to the Democratic Party and the Clinton Library. Rich may have indeed deserved the pardon, but the pardon deserved the scrutiny it received.

Perhaps the most infamous presidential pardon was granted to a president himself, when Gerald Ford pardoned his disgraced predecessor, Richard Nixon, for his criminal actions during the Watergate scandal. "I do believe," Ford announced, "that the buck stops here, that I cannot rely upon public opinion polls to tell me what is right. . . . If I am wrong, ten angels swearing I was right would make no difference." But in the end, "I feel that Richard Nixon and his loved ones have suffered enough." There were plenty who disagreed, but that's the power of the president. Or in this case, two presidents.

Presidential pardons aren't always so divisive. Every year just before Thanksgiving, the sitting president of the United States chooses to pardon a turkey, whether that turkey deserves it or not. (They can't all be innocent, can they?) It's fascinating to realize that every president since Harry Truman has been in the pocket of the Gobbler lobby. Talk about scandalous.

Now it was my turn.

At the end of my second and last term as governor of New Mexico, I considered a pardon with repercussions far greater than any simple Turkey-gate. In one of my most controversial actions as governor, I announced that I was contemplating a pardon of a young man named William Henry McCarty. The fascination among the press, the citizens of New Mexico, and the country over a possible pardon for McCarty was, to say the least, intense.

Why?

Because William Henry McCarty wasn't just William Henry McCarty. He was also known as William Bonney, and as Henry Antrim, and as Kid Antrim.

But his most famous nickname?

Billy the Kid.

I grew up with Billy the Kid. Which is to say, as a child I loved all stories of the Wild West and played sheriff and outlaw with all my friends. For obvious reasons—my name is Billy, after all, and I was a kid—I was cast as Billy the Kid in all of our backyard shoot-'em-ups. Just as it did for William McCarty, it became my nickname, too: Billy the Kid. To this day, my sister and my mother still call me that. Even decades later, when I was in Congress, a fellow congressman, Neil Abercrombie of Hawaii, loved hollering, "Hey, it's Billy the Kid!" whenever he saw me down the hallway. (My response, "Hey Abercrombie & Fitch!" wasn't nearly as historic, but hey, it was the best I could come up with.)

So who exactly was Billy? The Kid, who had been convicted for his part in the killing of a sheriff during the Lincoln County War, wasn't just another Wild West gunfighter. He was a folk superstar. Songs have been written about him. Movies made. He was an icon, a legend, and either a villain or a hero to many New Mexicans.

And as I prepared to leave office, he had been dead for 129 years.

Posthumous pardons aren't unheard of. Just a few weeks before his term ended in the same year as mine, Florida governor Charlie Crist pardoned Jim Morrison, the lead singer of the Doors, thirty-nine years after Morrison's death. Morrison had allegedly exposed himself onstage during a concert in Miami in 1969, which was apparently illegal even back in 1969. Accounts of the event vary, but it's not a huge stretch to believe that Morrison was guilty of the crime. Still, Crist thought enough time had passed that he felt comfortable clearing Morrison's name. That was just one of the most recent. There have been more than a hundred posthumous pardons, many given to people who had already been executed.

I had mentioned upon taking office in 2003 that I might be interested in reopening the case of Billy the Kid for one specific reason. My predecessor Lew Wallace, the governor of New Mexico during the Kid's short life, had supposedly offered the Kid a pardon, but for unknown reasons Wallace never delivered. It seemed imperative (to me) that I look into the matter to see if promised justice had been denied.

I hadn't expected the passions it stirred. Since one of the questions was the true identity of Billy the Kid, the sheriff of Lincoln County, which relies almost entirely on Billy the Kid curiosity for its tourism, even began efforts to exhume the Kid and his mother to prove they were actually buried in Fort Sumner Cemetery. When I supported the decision to get to the bottom of the matter (so to speak), the mayor of Fort Sumner—perhaps only half-jokingly—warned me, "I'd think twice about coming back to Fort Sumner, Governor. You might get shot by Billy the Kid fans!"

Lucky for me, a judge ruled against giving the sheriff permission to dig up the Kid, and I decided to drop the issue. It's fair to say that, as governor of the fifth-largest state in square mileage—we make up much of the Wild West, after all—I got busy with making sure my beloved home remained the Land of Enchantment under my watch. There was a lot to do.

But I never forgot about Billy.

In 2010, as I neared the end of my second—and constitutionally final—term as governor, I considered whether to revisit a pardon for the Kid. I wasn't sure. It had aroused strong opinions on both sides seven years earlier. Should I kick this hornet's nest again?

There was another reason I hesitated. Honestly, although I had had a great deal of fun researching Billy's life and weighing the pros and cons of a pardon during my governorship—it's fair to say I had become a Billy historian—I wondered if the people I served would deem it too silly a cause. A historically fascinating case, sure, but something of a sideshow. And honestly, I had gotten a reputation as a governor who was perhaps too open-minded to some of my citizens' nuttier suggestions.

Take Roswell.

Even those far afield from New Mexico know that Roswell, the city in southeastern New Mexico, has its share of mysteries. It began on July 7, 1947, when some airborne vessel, by some descriptions a flying saucer, or a "flying disk," according to the field officer who reported it, crashed nearby. The US Army insisted it was nothing more foreign (or alien) than a weather balloon, but since the balloon had been deployed as part of their top secret Project Mogul, they couldn't say anything more. But there are many—scientists and fabulists alike—who insist that it was a UFO as we've come to know it, complete with aliens aboard.

In 2004, not long after chairing the Democratic National Convention, I wrote something that I thought was rather innocuous in a foreword to a book: "The mystery surrounding this crash has never been adequately explained—not by independent investigators, and not by the U.S. government. . . . Clearly, it would help everyone if the U.S. government disclosed everything it knows. . . . The American people can handle the truth—no matter how bizarre or mundane." Suddenly, I was the hero of the UFO crowd, and the villain to skeptics of such things.

In the hoopla, my greater point may have been lost: that conspiracies like these arise because the Department of Defense isn't entirely straightforward about what *did* happen. In any event, judging by the response from the it's-not-a-UFO contingent, you'd have thought I was wearing a tinfoil hat when I wrote it. My favorite response, which came from a professor at Foothill College in California: "This continues to confirm that election or appointment to high office does not guarantee wisdom in all areas of human thought."

I'm not sure I agree on the wisdom question. As I had to remind the Roswell Chamber of Commerce more than once, *You guys got a great thing going here. You oughta ham this up a bit.* For reasons unbeknownst to me—and the tourists who stream into Roswell looking for signs of alien life—they were very sensitive about it all.

But sure enough, when I was vetted for vice president, the vetters called everybody around, asking if I was a UFO nut.

So the question remained: Should I cap off my governorship by invoking a ghost? Everyone directly involved in the case of Billy the Kid was long buried. I worried that if I decided to go forward with the reconsideration of the Kid's pardon, soon my detractors would be sending Ouija boards to the Governor's Mansion. Predictably, as she prepared to take over the governor's office, my reactionary, vindictive successor Susana Martinez tried to gain points by claiming she wouldn't focus on such trivial matters, and that considering a pardon for the Kid would be "a waste of time." But it was easy to dismiss her complaining; she doesn't understand or appreciate the deep veins of culture and history that course through New Mexico.

The choice was mine, and mine alone, and I couldn't help thinking that I needed to do it. Who knew that it would result in one of the most intense personal negotiations I've ever had.

At the height of his gun-totin' misdeeds, Billy the Kid was exactly that: a kid. But by all accounts he started as a law-abiding, well-behaved child who did what he was told and respected his elders. His first employer—the manager of a neighborhood hotel who had taken him in at age fourteen after Billy's mother died—was supposedly surprised that Billy didn't steal from him like all the other kids had. When Billy the Kid was just a kid, he was an obedient and pleasant foster child who caused no trouble.

It wouldn't last.

A year later, supposedly inspired by the outlaws he read about in dime-store novels, the Kid was arrested in Grant County for stealing cheese. A few months after that, he was arrested again when found in possession of clothes stolen from a Chinese laundry. When he made a daring escape from behind bars by shinnying up the jailhouse chimney, his legend was born.

He was on the run from that moment on.

The Kid was at times both law enforcer and outlaw, killing the deserving and innocent alike. Although his exploits may be exaggerated in the retelling, legend has it he killed twenty-one people—one for every year of his life, as he was killed at the young age of twenty-one. According to one report of his death, he stumbled into a darkened room at Fort Sumner where Pat Garrett, the new sheriff of Lincoln County, happened to be sitting. In the low light, the Kid asked, *"¿Quién es?"* Garrett recognized the Kid's voice, and fired two shots. One hit the wall behind Billy. One hit the mark.

Billy the Kid never became Billy the Man.

But his legend grew for a century. Even though the Kid started his killing spree in Arizona, New Mexico has rightfully claimed him as ours. Heck, during my time as governor, our state's official Web site promoted a six-day self-guided Billy the Kid tour that ended by Fort Sumner's evocatively named Stinking Spring, where Garrett finally got his man. (If only we were so entrepreneurial about Roswell!)

So as New Mexico's chief executive I felt a special obligation to consider whether to reconsider a pardon for the Kid. My state's tourism board didn't want me to. They thought I'd be upsetting the applecart; specifically, they worried that we might have to unearth the Kid's grave, and even they admitted there was a chance he might not be there. Hard to promote that.

But I kept coming back to the one compelling reason to move ahead: the promise made by Governor Lew Wallace.

As it happens, Wallace was as colorful a character as the Kid. He was a general in the Union Army and the United States minister to the Ottoman Empire, and he later went on to write *Ben-Hur*, the best-selling novel of the nineteenth century. Not a shabby résumé.

Before the Kid's death—according to most accounts, anyhow—the pair had entered into an arrangement whereby the Kid would testify against others involved in the Lincoln County War and, in return, he'd be granted full amnesty. Wallace was alleged to have said, "In return for doing this, I will let you go scot-free with a pardon in your pocket for all your misdeeds." There was one misdeed above all others that the Kid needed pardoned: his part in the murder of Lincoln County sheriff William Brady, for which the Kid had been sentenced to hang.

However, Wallace never delivered on his alleged promise, and the Kid went back to his outlaw ways. I had to answer the question: Was the pardon still in his pocket?

By most accounts, Wallace had made the promise, even though no written proof exists. The preponderance of hearsay evidence suggested as much. As governor of New Mexico—the same position that Wallace had held—I felt it was my duty to determine if the promise had been made, and if so, why it hadn't been delivered on. If Wallace had made the promise, I was the man now in the governor's office, so it might be up to me to deliver on it. And in 2010, with only a few months left in my second term in office, I announced that I'd look into the matter in earnest. I even hinted that we might make a full spectacle of it, just for kicks: a mock trial at the Billy the Kid exhibit in Ruidoso, complete with period costumes—the whole nine yards. Randi McGinn, the most prominent trial lawyer in New Mexico, agreed to take up the case pro bono and advocate on behalf of a pardon for Billy the Kid. The BBC asked if they could film it. We were going to make a meal of it.

Then all hell broke loose.

To be honest, never had I expected such attention for what I'd thought was a fun way to make history come alive. Certainly I knew there would be local interest, but we got calls from Berlin, Tokyo, Moscow, South Africa, and South America. It turned out that Billy the Kid stirred passions all over the world. Have gun, will travel, indeed.

Locally, of course, the Kid wasn't just a legend. The names Garrett and Wallace weren't just names in the index of a textbook. To some, they were relatives. "Great-grandpa." "Great-uncle Lew." And although not every claim made of the Kid's patronage was bona fide, we heard from enough New Mexicans who had a vested interest in him that ultimately, amid claims that the full spectacle might be insensitive, we dropped the idea of the mock trial. But I insisted that we should still consider a pardon for the Kid.

And the negotiation began.

Actually, there were two negotiations. The first negotiation was with myself: I had to decide whether I believed Wallace had offered an immunity deal to the Kid. I also had to determine why that promise hadn't been kept.

It may sound strange to say "I had to negotiate with myself," but that's exactly what happens sometimes. I'm not sitting across from myself at some conference table (or plate of barbecued goat) in my mind. But it's legitimate: *What consequences do I face depending on which decision I make? What do I gain? What do I lose?* I'm sure you've had internal conversations like this with yourself many times. But what's the secret to "winning" a standoff in your own brain? For me, it comes down to being honest about the facts, and the impact of those facts. Objectivity is a hard thing to come by in your own mind. But you have to play it through.

The second negotiation was with the community. Just the mention that I might pardon Billy opened the floodgates. It became a huge story not only in New Mexico but also nationally, and I started being lobbied from all sides.

To be honest, I can't say it was entirely helpful in making my decision for the reason that it was an evenly divided response. As many people were for it as were against it. Op-eds in the national press were split. In the *New York Times*, Hampton Sides wrote that "regardless of whether he got a raw deal, the Kid was a thug." He also wondered if, after I had taken "significant steps forward with investments in solar and wind power, film production, and light rail," I had suddenly "lost [my] mind." Even my absent mind tells me that's an opinion held by a historian with exactly zero sense of occasion, or of the merits of making history come alive. On the other coast, in the *Los Angeles*

Times, Kid biographer Mark Lee Gardner wrote, "A deal is a deal, and 129 years doesn't change that. Billy is owed a pardon."

It got personal, and understandably so. I heard from the descendants of Pat Garrett, the lawman who ultimately shot the Kid. In a letter, they made their case clear: "If Billy the Kid was living amongst us now," they asked, "would you issue a pardon for someone who made his living as a thief and, more egregiously, who killed four law enforcement officers and numerous others?" It was a fair point. They also made the interesting and compelling case that if I were to pardon Billy, wouldn't that suggest their ancestor had killed a (relatively, at least) innocent man?

On the second point, I was careful to reassure them that wouldn't be my conclusion, and my deputy chief of staff Eric Witt made it crystal clear: "We consider Pat Garrett a true hero of the West."

A meeting with five members of the extended family of the slain sheriff, William Brady, was congenial and polite. However, in a statement released to the press, they made it clear, in no uncertain terms, that if I should pardon the Kid, they threatened to launch a virulent campaign to soil my name. I won't say I was intimidated, but I will say I was listening. It seemed excessive, but they got my attention.

I heard from Lew Wallace's descendants as well. William Wallace, former *New York Times* reporter and great-grandson of the governor, said a pardon would be "without any rational reasoning" and would reduce his ancestor from legendary hero of the West to a "dishonorable liar." I disagreed on both counts. I was taking stock of all the evidence carefully and rationally, and would be casting no aspersions on the former governor. But I was more than happy to take Wallace's heartfelt views into consideration. He wrote that if I were to pardon the Kid, my action would "desecrate, defile, debase and dishonor" his great-grandfather. While I admired the amount of alliteration, I definitely disagreed with the details.

I was lobbied as well by Randi McGinn, the esteemed trial attorney who had agreed to take up the case pro bono. She too thought there was merit in revisiting the question of whether Lew Wallace had struck a deal with the Kid that was not delivered on. Her argument? "A promise is a promise and should be enforced," she wrote.

Amusingly, I also heard from people around the state and around the world who claimed to be descendants of Billy the Kid himself. Absent a DNA match, that would have been hard to prove, and rather unbelievable. There is no record of the Kid having any children in any of his twenty-one years. Though I admit it's possible; I suppose it depends on how wild his West was.

Members of the general public weighed in, of course, and I was happy to hear what they had to say. It had become a tradition in my office to keep an open-door policy—one probably far more open than most executives have. I had even implemented what I called "Five Minutes with the Governor." Throughout my term as governor, once every two months I'd set aside three hours in the morning and three hours in the afternoon when everyday New Mexicans could come in and negotiate with me on whatever subject they cared to. (Even when I was in Congress, I was similarly available. I once held twelve town halls in one day, infuriating Al Gore, who prided himself on being the most accessible, and ultimately I held more town meetings than any other member of Congress.) Many of those conversations were about the Roswell conspiracy and the pardon of Billy the Kid. As I recall, one person had a theory that the two were related. (I can't recall the details. Maybe the Kid shot down the UFO? As I said, almost anyone could visit my office, whether they turned out to be delusional or not.)

This was different from the other negotiations I've described in this book. For the most part, those involved face-to-face bargaining sessions with each party looking for a particular outcome. And those cases required their own sets of strategies. In this case, however, as the governor, my decision would determine the outcome of a given situation. I had the final word. That meant that everyone had to come to me. And multiple parties—indeed, thousands of individuals—all wanted to have their say. And their way. This is how leaders "negotiate" with the people they lead. I had to listen. And listen. And listen. The many points of view were legit, and they all mattered. If this would be my last act as the governor of New Mexico, I wasn't about to half-ass it.

As the clock ticked down to New Year's Eve, which would be the last day of my service as governor, we opened up the governor's Web site to public comment. More than a thousand chose to make their voices heard, and although a slight majority was in favor of a pardon, the essentially evenly split decision among the public didn't make making *my* decision any easier. New Mexicans wanted to forgive, perhaps as a way of not forgetting. But I didn't have the luxury of just clicking a box. Ironically, what had begun as a fun exercise in reawakening history had started to truly weigh on me. I was still enjoying myself, but it had become serious business.

Two of my closest advisors, Eric Witt and Alarie Ray-Garcia, were on this journey with me. Between the three of us, we had every angle covered, and we had become more than armchair experts in Billy the Kid. But even they were divided on the matter: Eric was for a partial pardon ("Billy got rooked"), while Alarie was against it ("Wallace must have changed his mind for a reason"). I asked them to draft memos laying out their best arguments, and both were candid and compelling. Eric saw Wallace's verbal promise of a pardon as authentic and immutable. "Your word is your bond," he wrote, "and that doesn't change with time." Still, he called for a partial pardon for only the death of William Brady, pointing out that "He'll burn in hell for the rest."

Alarie played to my heartstrings, explaining that "I'm a native New Mexican. Please don't tamper with our history." She also put my own place in history into stark perspective. "The story [of Billy the Kid] is so iconic and legendary," she wrote, "that I don't think it should be tampered with by anyone—even you."

I had to laugh. They knew me too well.

The world was watching. I knew there was no way to put the genie back in the bottle, so when George Stephanopoulos called to ask if I would make my pardon announcement on *Good Morning America*, I agreed. Even though, with only a few dozen hours left to spare, I still didn't know what I planned to say.

We closed the office on December 30. That night, I took Eric and Alarie out to dinner. I don't remember what we ate, but I certainly remember what we discussed: Billy, of course. Then we went back to the Governor's Mansion to continue the deliberations. Most of the furniture had already been moved out, but we found a few chairs and debated the pros and cons yet again late into the night. Midnight came and went and December 31 arrived—the day of reckoning. I knew I had to get up at 3:30 a.m. in order to make the *GMA* interview in time. And speaking honestly, as I laid my head down on the pillow, I wasn't certain about what I was going to do. *Perhaps*, I hoped, *a few hours' sleep will make it all clear.*

Just to be prepared, we had drafted two press releases—

one announcing a pardon, one declining the pardon—in much the same way candidates for office often have two speeches prepared on election day. One for victory, one for concession. I even asked that the official pardon be drafted so that if I went through with it, the matter could be handled efficiently. (Also, since the governor's office was closed, I worried that we wouldn't be able to get it completed by the time of *"Auld Lang Syne"*!)

The next morning, I made my decision, but I told no one my plans. Even my trusted aide Eric Witt wasn't sure what I had in mind. "I remember watching you on TV and thinking you'd do it," he told me later.

I didn't do it.

As history recalls, I did not pardon Billy the Kid. Although I was inclined to finish the work that Wallace had not—and I did conclude that the promise of a pardon had been made—I couldn't overlook a few facts. First, the pardon, although promised, was never granted. Why not? I had to allow for the fact that there may have been extenuating circumstances. Perhaps there had been more to Billy's side of the deal than just testimony, and perhaps he hadn't lived up to those obligations. Or perhaps Billy had violated other conditions of the pardon. It was impossible to know. And second, after Wallace reneged on the pardon, and after the Kid concluded a pardon wasn't in the offing, he had killed two innocent lawmen as he made yet another daring escape from the Lincoln County jail. Of course my pardon wouldn't have been for those killings, but the public seemed to be confused on that matter, and it would be difficult to explain that to everyone I met. It had to weigh in the decision.

So I made my announcement. "It was a very close call," I told ABC correspondent Bill Weir. "I've been working on this for eight years." And while "the romanticism appealed to me to issue a pardon . . . the facts and the evidence did not support it."

In the end, William Henry McCarty, aka William Bonney, aka Billy the Kid, may have been a multinamed marquee draw for the state of New Mexico, but he was also a murderer.

Although I had begun this process in part because I thought it would be "fun," in my official statement, we tried to be as respectful as possible to all parties involved, while still noting that the legend had only grown with our attention to it. "Billy the Kid is not dead," we wrote. "He remains very much alive in the culture, history, and imaginations of the public to this day. Not just in New Mexico, but throughout the country and around the world. . . . However, pardons are serious business. History is serious business. If one is to rewrite a chapter as prominent as this, there had better be certainty to the facts, the circumstances, and the motivations of those involved. . . . The point is, I don't know for sure. No one does. . . . Therefore I am not in a position at this time to issue a pardon for Billy the Kid. History lives on."

So I suppose it's official: You can add a dead gunslinger to the list of famous people I've negotiated with. Each one of the situations in this book, as you've seen, taught me a lot. I hope you learned something as well. I was careful (sometimes to my chagrin) to show you foul-ups as well as successes. The Billy the Kid situation remains dear to my heart to this day, however, mostly because I think I did that one right from start to finish—including my decision to leave Billy hanging, so to speak.

Maybe that's the last lesson here. After you negotiate with anyone—colleague, enemy, friend, family, nutty neighbor—you'll always be tempted to look back and wonder about the outcome. Even if you "won," could you have done better? If you didn't get what you wanted, what went wrong? Remember, there's nothing wrong with a little hindsight. That's how you learn.

And hey, it's also how you end up with a head full of

interesting stories. Negotiating may seem on the surface to be a black-and-white process. But trust me, life's better when it's colorful.

Many people to this day think Billy the Kid got a raw deal. One in particular sticks with me. On New Year's morning, Eric Witt and I went to breakfast at one of my favorite spots, Tia Sophia's in Santa Fe. As I sat there, relieved that the decision had been made and, if I'm being honest, a little exhausted after eight years as governor, an old man sidled up to me. He was a true Spanish *viejo*, about as authentic a New Mexican as you can get. By the looks of the wrinkles on his face, he could have been a contemporary of Billy's, impossible though that was. With no malice, with just the certainty earned by having lived a long life, he simply said, "I think you should have pardoned him." I nodded politely and let him have the last word.

For once, I was through negotiating.

The *viejo* ambled away, and even though it was morning, I'm pretty sure he walked into the sunset.

ACKNOWLEDGMENTS

GOV. BILL RICHARDSON

In preparing this book I want to especially commend my collaborator, Kevin Bleyer, for his enormous skills and his outsized personality. I want to thank my editor, Mike Zimmerman, for his encouragement, practicality, and his unique ability to make sure the trains ran on time. I am also forever grateful for my friend and agent provocateur Marc Adelman for putting me together with Rodale.

Speaking of which, many thanks must go to the Rodale family and the team at Rodale Books: Mary Ann Naples, Jennifer Levesque, Kara Plikaitis, Nancy Bailey, Nancy Elgin, Yelena Nesbit, Aly Mostel, and Brent Gallenberger.

In addition I am indebted to my former aides and advisers who contributed valuable recollections for the manuscript: Calvin Humphrey, Rebecca Gaghen, Mickey Bergman, Mike Stratton, Eric Witt, Tony Namkung, Allan Oliver, and Alarie Ray-Garcia. And to my trusted aide Caitlin Kelleher, who has been at my side for the past year since I started the book.

Thanks must also go to dear friends who have stood by me: Brian Condit, Mary Brophy, Brooke Lange, Nacho Vazquez, Peter Schoenburg, Randi McGinn, Jay Rosenblum, Greg Craig, Bob and Bylle Redford, Cliff Sloan, Margery Kraus, Dave Contarino, Janis Hartley, Mack McClarty, Steve Cozen, Amanda Cooper, and Manuel Sanchez Ortega.

And finally, I could not have written this book without the help of three extraordinary women: my wife, Barbara; my sister Vesta; and my mother, Maria Louisa, who died last year.

KEVIN BLEYER

Thanks go first, foremost, and finally to the master negotiator himself, Bill Richardson, for being such a skilled storyteller, a true confidant, a good friend, and an indefatigable tour guide. I know it's far too common a sentiment, but: There is no one with whom I'd rather stare at the embalmed corpse of Kim Jong-il.

It's a fool's errand to catalogue all the people who helped with this book, but since I am a fool: Thanks to our fellow traveling companions Mickey Bergman, John Delury, Jared Cohen, and Sophie and Eric Schmidt. Thanks to the Governor's devoted staff and advisers over the years, including Caitlin Kelleher, Alarie Ray-Garcia, Eric Witt, Brooke Lange, Rebecca Gaghen, Allan Oliver, and the estimable Calvin Humphrey. Thanks to the Governor's lovely wife, Barbara, for one delicious meal and a dozen delicious stories. Thanks to the shrewd scalpel and smart pen of editor Mike Zimmerman and the team at Rodale. A debt is also owed to Stephen Perrine and Marc Adelman for thinking of me for this project in the first place. I'd also like to thank Fidel Castro, Hugo Chavez, Saddam Hussein, three different Kims, the traffic ladies of Pyongyang, Billy the Kid, the aliens at Roswell, and all the dictators, despots, and divas who appear in this pages, if only because I can't think of another book under heaven and earth where I'd have that opportunity. Perhaps the sequel.

INDEX